THE HAMLYN LECTURES
FORTY-NINTH SERIES

COMMERCIAL LAW IN THE NEXT MILLENNIUM

AUSTRALIA
LBC Information Services—Sydney

CANADA and USA
Carswell—Toronto

NEW ZEALAND
Brooker's—Auckland

SINGAPORE and MALAYSIA
Thomson Information (S.E. Asia)—Singapore

COMMERCIAL LAW IN THE NEXT MILLENNIUM

by

PROFESSOR ROY GOODE
CBE, Q.C., LL.D., Hon. D.Sc. Econ. (Lond.), FBA

Published under the auspices of
THE HAMLYN TRUST

LONDON
SWEET & MAXWELL
1998

Published in 1998 by Sweet & Maxwell Limited of
100 Avenue Road, Swiss Cottage,
London NW3 3PF
Typeset by LBJ Typesetting Ltd of Kingsclere
Printed in England by
Clays Ltd, St Ives plc

No natural forests were destroyed to make this product;
only farmed timber was used and replanted

A CIP catalogue record for this book is available from the British
Library

ISBN 0 421 63650 5 (HB)
0 421 63660 2 (PB)

©
Roy Goode
1998

TABLE OF CONTENTS

Contents

THE HAMLYN LECTURES

The Hamlyn Lectures

The Hamlyn Lectures

The Hamlyn Lectures

THE HAMLYN TRUST

The Hamlyn Trust owes its existence to the will of the late Miss Emma Warburton Hamlyn of Torquay, who died in 1941 at the age of 80. She came of an old and well-known Devon family. Her father, William Bussell Hamlyn, practised in Torquay as a solicitor and J.P. for many years, and it seems likely that Miss Hamlyn founded the trust in his memory. Emma Hamlyn was a woman of strong character, intelligent and cultured, well-versed in literature, music and art, and a lover of her country. She travelled extensively in Europe and Egypt, and apparently took considerable interest in the law and ethnology of the countries and cultures that she visited. An account of Miss Hamlyn by Dr Chantal Stebbings of the University of Exeter may be found, under the title "The Hamlyn Legacy", in volume 42 of the published lectures.

Miss Hamlyn bequeathed the residue of her estate on trust in terms which it seems were her own. The wording was thought to be vague, and the will was taken to the Chancery Division of the High Court, which in November 1948 approved a Scheme for the administration of the trust. Paragraph 3 of the Scheme, which closely follows Miss Hamlyn's own wording, is as follows:

> "The object of the charity is the furtherance by lectures or otherwise among the Common People of the United Kingdom of Great Britain and Northern Ireland of the knowledge of the Comparative Jurisprudence and Ethnology of the Chief European countries including the United Kingdom, and the circumstances of the growth of such jurisprudence to the Intent that the Common People of the United Kingdom may realise the privileges which in law and custom they enjoy in comparison with other European Peoples and realising and appreciating such privileges may recognise the responsibilities and obligations attaching to them."

The Trustees are to include the Vice-Chancellor of the University of Exeter, representatives of the Universities of London,

Leeds, Glasgow, Belfast and Wales and persons co-opted. At present there are nine Trustees:

From the outset it was decided that the Trust's objects could best be achieved by means of an annual course of public lectures of outstanding interest and quality by eminent Lecturers, and by their subsequent publication and distribution to a wider audience. The first of these Lectures were delivered by the Rt Hon. Lord Justice Denning (as he then was) in October and November 1949; details of the subsequent Lectures may be found on pages vii–x. In recent years, however, the Trustees have expanded their activities by setting up a "small grants" scheme to provide financial support for other projects designed to further public understanding of the law. With a view to marking the 50th Series of Hamlyn Lectures, to be delivered in November 1998 by the Hon. Mr Justice Sedley, four special awards were recently made under this scheme, as follows:

- **Coatbridge CAB, North Lanarkshire:** to assist the creation and testing of a pilot scheme in the use of computers for improving the quality of information and advice given in the interview room (in conjunction with Citizens Advice Scotland);

- **Legal Services Agency Ltd, Glasgow:** to provide bursaries to enable social workers, lay advisers and other interested persons to attend seminars and workshops on social welfare, housing and mental health law;

- **Liberty, London:** to facilitate the setting up of a programme of training courses and seminars designed to improve the quality and effectiveness of advice given by advice workers in the public, community and voluntary sectors; and

- **Centre for Criminal Justice Studies, The University of Leeds:** to create a world-wide web site designed to promote understanding of the law and the legal system of the United Kingdom by means of accessible formats and non-technical language.

Further information relating to these projects is available from the Trustees.

The forty-ninth series of Hamlyn Lectures consisted of four lectures delivered by Professor Roy Goode on four successive Thursdays in November and December 1997; the first and last of these lectures were given in St John's College, Oxford, and the second and third were given in the Centre for Commercial Law Studies, Queen Mary and Westfield College, London.

March 1998   **DESMOND GREER**
                                        Chairman of the Trustees

PREFACE

When Professor Desmond Greer, the Chairman of the Trustees of the Hamlyn Trust, approached me with an invitation to deliver the 1997 Hamlyn Lectures, I felt honoured to be asked to join such a long line of distinguished predecessors, headed by that great judge Lord Denning, but daunted by the task. Commercial law, at least in the sense in which I have defined it, is a vast subject, drawing on the law of contract, tort, property, equity and trusts, and on public law; indeed, on all the streams of law that make up the corpus of English jurisprudence; and the Hamlyn Lectures are designed not for lawyers alone but for all those interested in the development of our law and legal institutions. The choice lay between selecting a particular aspect of the subject as my theme or surveying the field as a whole. With some hesitation I opted for the broad sweep, the panoramic view of the balloonist (my critics will no doubt say, a hot-air balloonist!) rather than the focused dig of the archaeologist. My aim has been to convey to a mixed audience and readership the sheer excitement of English commercial law: its history and its vigour; its combination of intellectual subtlety and remarkable responsiveness to the changing needs of the commercial community; the principles and policies that compete for its attention; and its future in an era characterised by technological change and the interdependence of markets and by the growth of what has become known as transnational commercial law.

The task of depicting all this within the confines of this slender volume—and I have consciously sought to keep it short and lightly footnoted so as to preserve the character of the lectures from which it is derived—has proved even more formidable than I had expected. Almost every issue discussed has been the subject of major textbooks and extensive analysis in periodic literature. I have endeavoured—with what success only my readers can judge—to capture the spirit of English

xv

commercial law and to focus on what seem to me to be its essential characteristics and points of stress.

The product is therefore a distillation of ideas that have undergone a long period of germination and have been garnered from a wide range of sources and from my own experiences in the course of a decidedly eccentric career. At the heart of private law governing commercial transaction lie the tensions between form and substance, between the strictness of contractual obligations and the principles of equity which moderate conduct in business life, between conceptual purity and commercial reality. The picture is no less complex in the field of public law, whose influence on commercial life is becoming all-pervasive, not only because of legislative regulation but because of judicial review of the decisions of public and quasi-public bodies and challenges to the *vires* of local authorities and statutory organisations. The role of public law will become more dominant still with the enactment of the European Convention on Human Rights, a development whose significance for business interests has yet to be appreciated by industry and commerce. Meanwhile, the relative merits of regulation and self-regulation, and of broad standards and detailed rules, continue to be debated. Finally, we have to ask ourselves whether, at the domestic level, our commercial law in general and our statute law in particular are adequate for the tasks ahead as we move towards the 21st century, and whether internationally the United Kingdom is not losing influence by its reluctance to codify its commercial law and to ratify international instruments to the shaping of which it makes such valuable contributions.

The challenges of the future are so much greater than those of the past because of the speed and scale of change: the increasing replacement of paper with electronic records, the problem of regulation in an era of globalisation, the amorphous character of the Internet, which allows contracts to be concluded by the press of a button before the parties are even known to each other, and through channels of communication that are often untraceable. Meanwhile, European Community law will continue to play an increasingly dominant role in the conduct of business.

I have no doubt that our commercial law will rise to these challenges, but if it is to do so successfully we must be much readier than we have shown ourselves in the past to look overseas and to learn from the experiences of lawyers and lawmakers in other jurisdictions. Many more of our scholars, even if not themselves comparative lawyers, are developing an interest in comparative law, whilst the House of Lords has, in recent years, set an example in its awareness of the value of resorting on occasion to the doctrine and jurisprudence not only of other common law systems but also of civil law jurisdictions. Of particular interest also is the remarkable impact of recent international and European restatements, such as the Unidroit Principles of International Commercial Contracts and its European counterpart, the Principles of European Contract Law prepared by the Commission on European Contract Law. Perhaps the warm response to these products of international academic collaboration also reflects a growing frustration at the unwillingness of governments to find legislative time to implement international conventions on the private law of international trade. Whatever the reason, we may be witnessing a return to the halcyon days of the medieval *jus commune* when it was left to the scholars, rather than the legislators, to systematise the law, and to courts to anchor that law in practicality through judgments which, in the words of Professor Raoul Van Caenegem, "are concerned with real people and real cases". One thing is certain: that in the future, as in the past, commercial law will be driven by and fashioned from the legitimate needs and practices of the mercantile community; for commercial law, above all, is a users' law, and it is from the creativity of the merchant and the financier in devising new instruments and new business methods that it will continue to evolve.

Roy Goode
St John's College
Oxford
March 29, 1998

ACKNOWLEDGMENTS

My first debt, is, of course, to the Hamlyn Trustees for inviting me to deliver the 1997 Hamlyn Lectures, and to their Chairman, Professor Desmond Greer, for the immense trouble he took over the arrangements and his exemplary patience in dealing with a lecturer all too prone to absent-minded disorder. I should also particularly like to thank Alison Seaman, a law student at the University of Essex, for all her research assistance and her rapid grasp of key issues. Her endeavours saved me a considerable amount of labour.

Every scholar builds on the work of his or her predecessors. Over the years I have benefited greatly from the writings of others, a number of which are referred to in the pages that follow, and from my discussions with academic and practising colleagues and debates with students. They are too numerous to list individually. To all of them I am deeply indebted. Stephen G. Austin, of Fulbright and Jaworski, was good enough to respond rapidly to my urgent request for a copy of his two-part co-authored article on the *Lykes Steamship* decision referred to on page 65.

The first and last of the Hamlyn Lectures took place at St John's College, Oxford, where hospitality was kindly provided by the international law firm Norton Rose and Sweet & Maxwell. The second and third lectures were given at my former academic home, Queen Mary and Westfield College, University of London, through the courtesy of the Principal, Professor Graham Zellick (now Vice-Chancellor of that University) and Professor Ian Fletcher, Director of the Centre for Commercial Law Studies. I am most grateful for the hospitality there extended by Ian Fletcher and the Centre, and by the Trustees of the Hamlyn Trust, and for all the arrangements so efficiently made by Ian Fletcher's personal assistant, Mildred Schofield; while at the Oxford end my secretary, Judith Crowle, was, as always, immensely helpful and hardworking. I should also like to express my thanks to the staff of Sweet & Maxwell for all their work in the editing, indexing and production of this book.

I must also record my deep indebtedness to Norton Rose for supporting the Chair of English Law over the past eight years. By arrangement with the University this support is being transferred to a newly established Chair, the Norton Rose Chair of Commercial and Financial Law, attached to St Hugh's College, while the University will resume responsibility for the funding of the Chair of English Law, to which Professor Paul Craig has been appointed as my successor upon my retirement at the end of the present academic year. So I will have been the first and last Norton Rose Professor of English Law, a post I have been privileged to hold since 1990 at St John's College, where I have spent eight happy years, through the kindness and support of the President, Dr William Hayes, the other Fellows and staff of the college and my friends and colleagues in the Faculty of Law. A special word of appreciation to college and University appears at the conclusion of the lectures. Finally, I must once again express my deep gratitude to my long-suffering wife Catherine, for her constant support and encouragement of a husband who has been all too prone to working at unsocial hours and to mislaying books and papers at crucial moments of authorship and lecturing. *Amantes amentes!*

R.M.G.

TABLE OF CASES

Table of Cases

TABLE OF STATUTES

TABLE OF STATUTORY INSTRUMENTS

The 1997 Hamlyn Lectures

In the history of the world few influences have been as powerful as the driving force of trade. The constant search for new markets impelled merchants to embark on vast voyages to the unknown, by land across the caravan routes linking West to East from Sardis in Anatolia through Samarkand to Tunhwang in China, and by sea around the Mediterranean and later to the Americas and Australasia. The picture is well captured by Sir Richard Atkin in his foreword to Wyndham Bewes' book *The Romance of the Law Merchant*.

"They whose lawful occasions bring them into the commercial courts of this country are not usually associated with romance; whereby they are doubtless spared much publicity. But the practitioners in such courts are accustomed to tales of adventure and hairbreadth escapes that might provide the material for bales of stories should any visitor from the world of literature stray thereto. There are tales told in the Admiralty Court almost daily of perils by sea, endurance, sacrifice, courage, resource of mariners, that may some day attract the reporters that flock to an adjoining court . . .

It is, perhaps fortunate that the law-makers of former days took little interest in the rules of commerce, provided that the results were such as to ensure that the sovereign lord had sufficient whereof to take toll. As a result, traders made their own rules and administered them summarily at their own courts, with the tacit or express approval of the Sovereign. Such rules have in the course of ages crystallised into law; in many cases recorded in statutory codes. The history of this growth takes us over the trade routes of Asia, transports us in the ships of Hiram with cargoes of gold and ivory, apes and peacocks, carries us in voyages along the Mediterranean and beyond, find us making voyages in the Euxine in joint adventure with Greeks . . . and will take us to all the fairs and markets of Europe; and expose us to the special customs of our own English towns."

The 1997 Hamlyn Lectures

This year's Hamlyn lectures seek to convey the spirit of English commercial law: the influences that have shaped it; the creativity of the merchants and their lawyers; the responsiveness and intellectual ingenuity of the judges; the tensions set up by competing legal policies and doctrines; and the future of commercial law as we approach the next millennium. Miss Hamlyn was anxious that her lecturers should inculcate a knowledge of comparative European jurisprudence among the common people of the United Kingdom, with the aim of demonstrating the superiority of English law. I would in any event have drawn on foreign sources by way of comparison, without which one can have only a very imperfect perception of one's own legal system; and if I have not fulfilled the latter part of her injunction it is because she died 32 years before this country joined the Common Market, and Miss Hamlyn would, I am sure, have been familiar with the principle *rebus sic stantibus*. In the development of our commercial law we have long been influenced by decisions in other major common law jurisdictions within the British Commonwealth, notably Australia, Canada, and New Zealand, as well as by legal developments in Canada's great trading partner, the United States. Our membership of the European Union has made us increasingly aware of the need to become more closely attuned to the rich legal cultures that form the bedrock of that great legal family, the civil law. The renowned John Donne once wrote: "No man is an island." Today we can go further and say: "No island is an island."

Some 48 years have elapsed since Lord Denning—who was to become one of England's greatest judges and is happily still with us—inaugurated this lecture series with his inspiring talks on *Freedom under the Law*. I should like to thank the trustees of the Hamlyn Trust for the privilege of being invited to deliver the 1997 Hamlyn lectures.

2

1. The Shaping of Commercial Law

I SKETCHING THE MAP

The evolution of commercial law

Commercial law has evolved from the needs and practices of the mercantile community; from opportunities to be grasped and problems to be overcome. It is these that have provided the impetus for new types of agreement, new contract structures, new instruments of trade. In some respects the launching of each fresh device has been almost as fraught with hazard as that of a long sea voyage. When it comes to the test, will the courts uphold the new instrument as achieving its intended purposes or will they strike it down, with the prospect of inhibition, or even ruination, of a flourishing market? It is a tribute to the good sense of the judges of old and their successors that, for the most part, they responded to the challenge in a positive and constructive way, through a relaxed approach to commercial contracts and a recognition of the importance of upholding reasonable market practice. It is in no small measure due to them that London can now fairly claim to be the world's leading financial centre.

It is a characteristic of human behaviour—some would say, of human folly—that we learn primarily from our own experiences, not from those of our predecessors. The history of commercial law is one of constant reinvention of the wheel. Thus the Italians are credited with inventing the bill of exchange, though its forerunner was in use in the ancient city of Karkemish in the seventh century before Christ.[1] English law takes credit for inventing the floating charge in the latter part of the 1800s, yet Roman law possessed a security not so very different in the shape of the *hypotheca*.

[1] W.A. Bewes, *The Romance of the Law Merchant* (1923), pp. 48 *et seq.*

This constant rediscovery of rules and techniques developed by our ancestors reflects a point of some importance, namely that commercial law evolves from the usages of business, so that the level of its influence and the degree of its subtlety at any one time are a function of the volume of economic activity and the complexity of the practices that drive commercial law. When a highly developed commercial community disappears, its laws and learning disappear with it. Such was the fate of the great Code of Hammurabi (itself derived in no small measure from the Sumerian laws), which, with the collapse of the Hammurabi dynasty, disappeared from view, not to be rediscovered, except in fragments and partial copies, until the lapse of some 3,800 years.[2] The sophistication of modern commercial law is thus a function of the size and interdependence of modern markets rather than of intellectual progression. Commercial law is about problem-solving, about fashioning the contract structures and other legal tools by which the legitimate needs of the market can be met.

By comparison with continental Europe, England was slow to develop a corpus of commercial law. It is true that we had a medieval law merchant. But its virtues lay primarily in the speed and informality of its processes, and its relaxed approach to evidence, rather than the development of substantive rules. English merchants lacked the autonomy and organisational structure of their continental colleagues, with their powerful guilds and their mercantile consuls. The civil law, with its concepts of fairness and good faith, might have exerted a greater influence if the Church and the Court of Admiralty, in which the civilians in Doctors' Commons practised and which applied the civil law, had not been curbed by the State and by the courts of common law, so that their jurisdiction was steadily eroded. Indeed, jurisdictional battles, and their periodic resolution by the courts, seemed to have almost as much significance as the development of substantive commercial law. This was true even in the 12 years of the Commonwealth, when the Protectorate by which we were governed introduced an Act

---

[2] See A.S. Diamond, *Primitive Law* (1935), Chap. IV; Driver and Miles (eds), *The Babylonian Laws*, Vol. I (1952), pp. 27 *et seq.* Diamond concluded (at pp. 1, 179) that the Code of Hammurabi, inscribed on a stela discovered by Jean-Vincent Scheil in 1901, represented a stage of legal development which was not reached in Rome until about 160 B.C. and in England until about A.D. 1250.

preserving the jurisdiction of the Court of Admiralty in matters relating to freight and bills of lading and other Admiralty matters[3] and an Ordinance removing the court's jurisdiction in actions on bills of exchange and accounts between merchants, whilst at the same time requiring each of the three judges to give reasons for his sentences.[4]

Modern historians now discount even the notion that the common law courts applied and absorbed the law merchant; rather, it is thought, did they receive evidence of commercial usage as fact and apply it directly, instead of borrowing from the law merchant.[5] So we must not allow ourselves to be too enslaved by the romance of the law merchant. If the medieval *lex mercatoria* laid the foundations, it is the central courts, particularly from the eighteenth century onwards, that have fashioned the body of principles and rules making up modern English commercial law.

A period of change

That an international *lex mercatoria* developed owes little to English merchants. Admiralty law drew heavily on such continental compilations as the Rolls of Oléron and the Consolato del Mare, which were copied into the Black Book of the Admiralty. In the evolution of international trade law the driving force was the Italian mercantile community, and it was from Italy, and from international transactions shaped by Italian usage, that England, like the rest of Europe, drew the inspiration for its own instruments of commerce, such as the bill of exchange and the bill of lading, and the foundations for its law of marine insurance.

How, then, has English commercial law attained its present eminence? I believe that at bottom there are three principal causes. The first is the huge growth of entrepreneurial activity,

[3] An Act for settling the Jurisdiction of the Court of Admiralty, July 30, 1653, printed in Firth and Rait, *Acts and Ordinances of the Interregnum 1648–1660*, Vol. 2, p. 712. Upon the Restoration the Acts and Ordinances of the Commonwealth were consigned to oblivion and do not feature in any official compilation of the statutes of the realm.
[4] An Ordinance for settling the jurisdiction of the Court of Admiralty, April 12, 1648, reprinted in *ibid.*, Vol. 1, p. 1120.
[5] See J.H. Baker, "The Law Merchant and the Common Law Before 1700" (1979) 8 C.L.J. 295; James Steven Rogers, *The Early History of the Law of Bills and Notes* (1995), pp. 1–2, 164 *et seq.*

in which many factors, including the law, have played a part. Commercial law derives its nourishment from commercial transactions. Without trading there would be no commercial law. London has been an international trading centre from Anglo-Saxon times.[6] The growth of capitalism and the competition for domestic and international business have led to a never-ending stream of new business instruments and techniques and to the evolution of specialist and sophisticated markets, each with its own communication system, its trading rules and its procedures for clearance and settlement. London has an international reputation for its highly developed specialist markets in commodities, short-term and long-term debt, equities, financial derivatives, foreign exchange, and transport and insurance services. These markets, the contracts they generate and the determination of the disputes that arise from them, form the bedrock of modern commercial law. London also benefits from an accident of geography, in that the country is happily located in a time zone that bridges the gap between New York and Tokyo.

The second cause is political and financial stability. Commercial law cannot flourish except in an environment which is financially stable and in which there is confidence in the organs of government and in the judiciary.

The third and crucial factor is the attitude of the legislature and the courts. If entrepreneurial activity is to be undertaken and to flourish, the legal system which accommodates it must be flexible and responsive to rapid change. Paternalism may give protection, but it stultifies initiative and inhibits the risk-taking and the receipt of profits which are essential to the health of a market economy. With the abandonment of mercantilism and the grant of overseas state trading monopolies, paternalism gave way to private enterprise. It is a fact that in the development of our legal techniques for the accommodation of business transactions the legislature has, rather remarkably, played almost no

---

[6] Not that the importance of its economy was always appreciated by the country's rulers, who in the Middle Ages regularly imposed heavy taxes and trading restrictions on London merchants, gave preferential treatment to foreign over local traders and, in a spectacular judicial murder by Parliament in 1338, had Sir Nicholas Brembre, four times mayor of London and one of its most masterful and dynamic leaders, drawn, hanged and quartered at Tyburn as a traitor. For a fascinating account of London's merchants in the Middle Ages, set in the context of the history of the Grocers' Company, see Pamela Nightingale, *A Mediaeval Mercantile Community* (1995).

part at all. A striking illustration of the non-interventionist policies of the State is that, except from some rather desultory provisions in the Bank Charter Act 1844, banking in the United Kingdom was not regulated by any legislation whatsoever until 1979. The whole system of control worked on the basis of the moral suasion exercised by the Governor of the Bank of England.

Now, as we approach the next millennium, we find commercial practice in a period of change unprecedented in its pace and scale. Transferable documents, heralded long ago as a breakthrough in facilitating dealings in goods, securities and money, have more recently been seen as a serious obstacle to progress as exporters, banks, exchanges and clearing systems found themselves engulfed by a tidal wave of paper, with all the attendant risk, cost of issue and storage, and delay and inconvenience of transmission. With the advent of new technology securities are becoming dematerialised or immobilised in depositary institutions; negotiable instruments are giving way to electronic funds transfers; physical cash will soon be displaced by the electronic purse; the paper-based bill of lading and letter of credit may one day be consigned to oblivion. Trading on the Internet is already with us, creating huge business opportunities but posing potentially enormous problems for law and for regulators. The increasingly abstract nature of markets, in which a variety of complex derivatives can be traded separately from the underlying physical transactions, raises in acute form the question how to distinguish trading and hedging from gambling and speculation. The conversion of non-tradable into tradable assets through securitisation brings in its train a sharper conjunction of consumer and commercial law than we have known in the past as consumer receivables become transferred into special purpose vehicles and unitised or given as security for public issues of notes and bonds. The so-called globalisation of the markets brings new challenges. Who should control activities of a corporation incorporated in one country which are conducted in another? Should we expect competition between regulators of different countries or a convergence of regulatory regimes?

Finally, both domestically and internationally commercial law is being profoundly influenced by political change. We have seen an almost worldwide movement from planned economies to mixed economies and from state control to privatisation, with important implications for the security of transactions and for the relative significance of public and private rights. Within the next few years we shall have monetary union in Europe, with or without the early participation of the United Kingdom, and we will have to confront the legal and political effects of the single currency.

The boundaries of commercial law

One of the distinctive features of the common law, which it shares with Roman law and, in recent times, with a few civil law jurisdictions, is that it makes no formal separation between the civil law and the law governing commercial transactions. There are no special rules for *commerçants* or requirements for them to be registered, nor is there any concept of *actes de commerce*, still less a commercial code, except in the United States. I shall have something to say in my final lecture about the nature of commercial codes and the utility of a commercial code for the United Kingdom. Suffice it to say for the moment that the absence of anything resembling either a commercial code or a commercial part of a civil code makes it particularly difficult to define the contours of the subject we so assiduously study, teach and practise.

Commercial law has traditionally been treated as a mere aggregation of specific subjects, such as sale, agency and negotiable instruments, each a self-contained field governed by its own distinctive rules.[7] But in truth commercial law is much more than this. In my own perception commercial law represents the totality of the law's response to mercantile disputes. It encompasses all those principles, rules and statutory provisions, of whatever kind and from whatever source, which bear on the private law rights and obligations of parties to commercial transactions, whether between themselves or in their relationship with others. Thus commercial law draws for its sustenance on all the great streams of law that together make up the corpus

---

[7] An honourable exception among writers was that remarkable legal scholar, barrister, statistician and actuary, Leone Levi, Professor of the Principles and Practice of Commercial Law at King's College London, whose two-volume book *International Commercial Law* (2nd ed., 1863) is a work of great erudition. Even Levi's smaller book on United Kingdom domestic law, *Manual of the Mercantile Law of Great Britain and Ireland* (1854) devotes the first three chapters to the progress of commerce, international commercial law and the nature, spirit and history of commercial law.

of English jurisprudence, with the law of contract as its core, whilst equity acts now as its handmaiden, now as the keeper of its conscience. The great judicial reformer Brougham was surely right to describe commercial law as "far purer and free from defects than any other part of the system."[8]

It follows that as our concepts of property and obligation expand and become more sophisticated in the light of commercial developments, so also does commercial law itself increase in scope and sophistication. And the growth of the law of obligations and the law of property in the past century has indeed been prodigious. The trust, from being essentially a family affair, now plays a crucial part in commercial life, both as a means of separating ownership and management and as a technique for co-ordinating fractional interests, such as those of the holders of publicly issued securities. We have seen an expansionist approach to the enforceability of promises, whilst liability for pure economic loss is now commonplace, even if its boundaries are controversial. Moreover, people seem unwilling any longer to accept the normal hazards of business life. If someone suffers loss or injury, someone else must pay.[9] All these developments have a direct impact on the rights and duties of parties to commercial transactions, and to this extent all of them can be regarded as sources of commercial law.

But perhaps the most remarkable partnership has been that between commercial law and equity. If contract lies at the heart of commercial law, it is equity that has provided the foundation for security interests in commercial assets and for the enhancement of the required standards of behaviour in the conduct of business life. In particular, the concept of fiduciary obligation has been significantly developed and refined, and there has been a marked shift from abstract rules to general standards which are fact-specific. Restitution, the reversal of unjust enrichment, has become accepted as an identified branch of law and is increasingly invoked as a remedy where there is no available claim in contract or where the benefits improperly received by the defendant exceed the amount of the plaintiff's recoverable loss. The relationship between the common law of contract and

---

[8] H.C. Deb., February 7, 1838, col. 130.

[9] Associated with this is the free-rider syndrome: an injured party should be entitled to ride on the back of obligations owed to and paid for by a third party.

the doctrines of equity mirrors the tensions between form and substance, and between predictability and justice in the individual case, and is a recurrent theme in modern commercial law.

We must also not overlook the importance of procedural law in these developments. The *Mareva* injunction and the *Anton Piller* order have developed into instruments of enormous power in the hands of plaintiffs concerned in the one case that the defendant may place his assets out of the reach of execution and in the other that evidence vital to the proof of infringement of intellectual property rights will disappear. As in substantive law there are compromises to be made: the protection of the plaintiff has to be set in the balance against the avoidance of oppression of the defendant. Increasingly our courts have come to see themselves as service providers in commercial disputes. Judicial case management is now being introduced, while the Commercial Court now not only requires the parties to consider alternative dispute resolution but offers its own neutral expert evaluation service.

The pre-eminence of dispositive law

If there is one feature above all that distinguishes English commercial law from that of civil law jurisdictions, it is the relative absence of mandatory law. The greater part of our commercial law is still to be found in jurisprudence rather than statute; and such legislation as we have governing commercial transactions is largely of a codifying and dispositive character, as, for example, the Bills of Exchange Act 1882 and the Sale of Goods Act 1979. This reflects a deeply-felt sense that if entrepreneurial activity is to be undertaken and to flourish, the legal system that accommodates it must be flexible and responsive to rapid change. Hence the role of statute is primarily to lay down a balanced set of rights and duties that will apply in default of agreement; that of the courts is to respect and enforce reasonable mercantile practice while refusing recognition to agreements offensive to public policy.

Let us consider for a moment the range of commercial instruments in current use. We have a battery of consensual security devices: the pledge, the mortgage, the fixed and floating charge, and the contractual lien. We have the express trust, widely used in commercial transactions. In the words of Oliver Wendell Holmes:

"Put not your trust in money, but put your money in trust."[10]

We have priority and subordination agreements, contractual set-off, retention of title under sale agreements. We can divide up or transfer rights in tangibles and intangibles, horizontally or vertically, by legal or equitable co-ownership, by trust and sub-trust, by assignment and sub-assignment, by syndication and participation. We have the concept of negotiability for bills of exchange, bearer securities, and certificates of deposit. We can also provide in advance for the automatic substitution of contracting parties by novation—an invaluable tool for increasing liquidity and reducing risk—and for the conferment of irrevocable powers of attorney, a common contractual device to allow assignees and secured creditors to perfect their title. The derivatives market has given rise to a wondrous array of contractual and securitisation devices which enable market participants to package financial assets, loans and investments in whatever way best suits their needs to secure such benefits as hedging, arbitrage, reduction of balance sheet assets and the minimisation of tax liabilities. And, astonishingly, not a single one of these commercial devices was the creature of statute. All of them evolved through commercial practice and were blessed by decisions of our judges; and what the common law lacked, equity in its beneficence was able to provide. Moreover, the law largely leaves it to the parties to agree on remedies, including repossession, sale and the appointment of an administrative receiver, which do not necessitate any recourse to the courts at all.

A civil lawyer would surely find this truly astounding. This ability of the parties to fashion security rights of their choice, to decide on other rights and remedies, and to exercise them without the need for recourse to the courts is peculiar to the common law and is nowhere more freely available than under English law. It is this freedom, coupled with an efficient and informal mechanism for the resolution of disputes in the commercial court, which in my belief accounts for the regular choice of English law by foreign parties in contracts which have no necessary conection with England at all. And it is the reconciliation of this same freedom with the need to secure the integrity

[10] *The Autocrat of the Breakfast Table* (2nd ed., 1903), Chap. II. The author of this engaging work was the famous judge's father.

11

of market practice that poses one of the greatest challenges to our commercial law.

II THE PHILOSOPHICAL FOUNDATIONS OF COMMERCIAL LAW

Commercial law and commercial morality

The relationship between law and morals is one which has exercised philosophers and jurisprudence scholars for a very long time. It causes particular difficulty in the field of commercial law, where the practice makes the law and is rooted in competition and freedom of contract.

Conduct which is morally culpable is more likely to be held a breach of duty than conduct which is morally blameless. To that extent, law and morality go hand in hand. It follows that changes in the moral climate which result in previously acceptable behaviour becoming labelled ethically unacceptable will in some degree, though not by the same measure, lead to changes in the judicial perception of what is lawful. So the *laissez-faire* approach, which led courts in the past to see nothing wrong in knockout agreements between dealers by which they undertook not to bid against each other at auction,[11] or the non-disclosure of relevant facts by directors in transactions with individual shareholders,[12] would undoubtedly be viewed in a quite different light by today's judges, who are more closely attuned to the concept of creating a false market. But if ethics influences law, the converse is also true. When once a practice that was previously lawful is rendered illegal it may also come to be perceived as morally wrong. The taint of illegality carries with it a sense of ethical impropriety that was previously absent. Examples are not hard to find: price-fixing; insider trading; concealed concert parties for the acquisition of control of a company.

Even so, the courts have continued to observe the distinction between breaches of law and breaches of moral obligation. A person is not required to be ethical or high-minded in mere social relationships falling outside the purview of legal responsibility, nor even in duty relationships where the position of the

---

[11] *Rawlings v. General Trading Co.* [1921] 1 K.B. 635.
[12] *Percival v. Wright* [1902] 2 Ch. 421.

parties is essentially adversarial and governed by considerations of mutual self-interest. Only where the relationship between the parties or the nature of the agreed arrangements involves one party having to repose trust and power in the other does the higher standard of behaviour set by equity come into play. It may be unethical to impose unfair contract terms but English contract law knows no general duty to be fair, nor, indeed, in commercial transactions is any such duty enshrined in statute. Bargains will not be struck down merely because they are very hard on one party and very favourable to the other; and this is so whether the imbalance of interest exists from the outset or is brought about by change of circumstances. Indeed, English contract law remains little concerned with substantive unfairness; its main emphasis is on procedural unfairness, impropriety in the manner in which bargains are induced—such as misrepresentation, non-disclosure of material facts in certain types of contract—and the exercise of duress or undue influence.

The courts are right to maintain the boundary between unethical and unlawful behaviour, if only because the conception of what is ethical varies so much from person to person and from case to case. This is particularly true of the duty of disclosure. Take the problem posed two thousand years ago by Cicero and derived from a test case propounded by the successors of Panaetius[13]:

> "Suppose that there is a food-shortage and famine at Rhodes and the price of corn is extremely high. An honest man has brought to the Rhodians a large stock of corn from Alexandria and he has seen their ships making for Rhodes with substantial cargoes of grain. Ought he to tell the Rhodians this? Or is he to say nothing and sell his stock at the best price he can get?"

I shall not attempt to answer this question tonight. Suffice it to say that it divided the leading philosophers of the day; and if they could not agree on the existence of a moral duty to disclose, it is scarcely surprising if the courts are reluctant to impose a legal duty to do so outside defined types of situation or relationship.

Yet the boundary between law and morality has become blurred because of a huge growth in the conferment of

---

[13] *On Duties, III*, Cicero, *Selected Works* (Penguin Classics, trans. Michael Grant, 1971 revision), pp. 177 *et seq*.

discretionary powers on courts and on a wide range of regulatory bodies. This is a matter to which I shall return next week. My focus tonight is on two sets of tension in commercial law: between predictability and justice and between form and substance.

Predictability versus justice

A recurrent theme in the development of English commercial law is the importance attached to predictability. As our judges have said again and again over the past 300 years, it is better that the law should be certain than that in every case it should be just. Businessmen have to order their affairs on the basis of a reasonable degree of continuity in legal thinking, and if judges were too ready to apply their notions of justice in the individual case this could upset not only the particular transaction in dispute but all comparable transactions. Indeed, the evolution of standard contracts and standard business structures to accommodate huge volumes of business makes it all the more necessary that the outcome of disputes should be reasonably predictable in the typical case.

Predictability requires, so far as possible, that contracts be given effect according to their natural meaning, allowing for any special meaning given by trade usage, and are not construed to produce effects manifestly against the intention of the parties. Predictability also demands the freedom of parties to require strict compliance in commercial dealings. Thus punctual adherence to stipulations as to the time of delivery and the time of payment is important in the commercial world, particularly in an era where contracts themselves are traded, so that an April shipment contract is of a different description from a May contract, and where markets are sometimes highly volatile, so that even a short delay can cause substantial loss. This approach is strictly applied. In *The Brimnes*,[14] for example, instructions were sent by a London bank to its New York correspondent at 10.53 a.m. to make an in-house payment to the defendants in respect of hire due from the plaintiffs the previous day as charterers under a charterparty. This being 4.53 a.m. New York time, the bank in New York was, of course, closed, and its staff slept on in blissful ignorance of impending disaster for the

[14] [1973] 1 All E.R. 769.

14

plaintiffs. The in-house transfer was estimated to have been completed some 20 minutes after the defendant, the owner of the vessel, had terminated the charterparty for default in payment. The termination was thus held valid and the plaintiffs lost the charterparty: a hard but necessary decision.[15]

Predictability does not, however, mean the absence of change. If it did, we should have no commercial law worthy of the name. Moreover, it is obvious that decisions given in one age against a background of prevailing commercial instruments and practice and a prevailing sentiment as to what is and is not proper cannot be allowed to restrict legal development in a later age, when the practices have changed and the perceptions of proper behaviour have become more refined. It is, indeed, an inevitable feature of legal development in any society with stable government that over time the legally required standard of behaviour increases, partly because more important matters, such as survival of the society, can be taken for granted, leaving more time to consider lower-grade issues, and partly because the ever-increasing sophistication of commercial practice brings in its train a correspondingly more sophisticated approach to regulation. I have remarked earlier that most of our commercial law is judge-made; and what the judges have created they are free to change to reflect new social or economic considerations or to correct principles or rules that can now be seen to have been mistaken. There is nothing fundamentally incompatible between respect for judicial precedent and judicial creativity. And if we seek proof of that proposition we need go no further than call to mind the great founder of English commercial law, Lord Mansfield. His encyclopaedic knowledge, reinforced by his practice of drawing on the expertise of the business community, enabled him to adapt the law to commercial needs in a remarkably creative fashion. His impact was such as to provoke a series of excoriating onslaughts from the pseudonymous author of *The Letters of Junius*:

"Who attacks the liberty of the press?—Lord Mansfield. Who invades the constitutional power of juries?—Lord Mansfield. What

---

[15] This was on the assumption that the New York bank's receipt of the money constituted acceptance by the owners and was not a mere ministerial act. In the light of subsequent authority this assumption was not in fact correct. See *Mardorf Peach and Co. Ltd v. Attica Sea Carriers of Liberia* [1977] A.C. 850. One's sympathy for the plaintiffs is muted by the fact that they had defaulted on previous occasions and had been warned of the consequences of any further late payment.

judge ever challenged a juryman, but Lord Mansfield? . . . Who is he, that has made it the study and practice of his life to undermine and alter the whole system of jurisprudence in the court of King's Bench?—Lord Mansfield."[16]

Yet Lord Mansfield himself was keenly aware of the importance of observing precedent—particularly where it favoured his own views—and of the danger of hard cases making bad law. What he strove to overcome in his age, as has Lord Denning in this century, was the sterility of legal reasoning which proceeded on the basis of precedent without principle and the application of technical rules without regard to legal policy or commercial usage. As Fifoot put it in his elegant biography:

> "The discovery of current usage by any appropriate method was not the last, nor the most delicate, function of the judge. When testimony had been sifted and the true faith found, it had still to be invested with doctrinal significance and incorporated into the law. It was precisely this process which Lord Mansfield's predecessors had shirked."[17]

What does cause concern is not change in itself but change which is made too readily or too frequently. Long-established principles should not lightly be given up. It is confusing if courts one year move in one direction, the next in another and in the third return to their starting position. But if change is properly controlled, the world of commerce will normally have little to fear.

Rules versus standards

Potentially more difficult for the commercial community is any major movement from rules to standards, from legal commands in which the content of the law is determined in advance to legal commands in which such content is given only at the point of decision by a judge or administrator[18] and on a case-by-case basis. Of course, the courts, like the legislation, have to lay down standards as well as rules. One of the most enduring has

---

[16] Letter of October 5, 1771, published as letter LIX in John Cannon (ed.), *The Letters of Junius* (Clarendon Press, 1978).

[17] C.H.S. Fifoot, *Lord Mansfield* (1977), p. 108.

[18] Louis Kaplow, "Rules versus Standards: An Economic Analysis" 42 Duke L.J. 557, 559–560 (1992).

been Lord Atkin's famous one-sentence statement in *Donoghue v. Stevenson* of the legal equivalent of the Biblical precept "love thy neighbour" as a way of defining to whom one owes a duty of care in tort.[19] In the context of physical injury or damage such a standard causes few problems; it is another matter when it comes to claims for pure economic loss.

The distinction between standards and rules does not, of course, remain clear cut, for courts and, to a lesser extent, tribunals, establish criteria by which standards are to be measured, in order to promote consistency in decision-making so that over time a standard tends to assume the characteristics of a rule.[20] Even so, it is evident that a decision which is fact-specific is considerably less predictable than one which is determined in advance by the rule and which thus depends only upon the rule's interpretation. Has the elevation of legal standards made the outcome of commercial disputes excessively unpredictable? I shall attempt to answer this question by examining the impact of principles developed in two fields: equity and the law of tort relating to liability for pure economic loss.

(1) Equity

It is often said that equity should have no significant role to play in commercial transactions, that the intervention of equity is inimical to the predictability which is so essential to commercial life. But businessmen and their lawyers who say this, in focusing on equitable duties, tend to overlook the enormous contribution made by equity to commercial rights. It is to equity that we owe one of the most highly developed systems of commercial security in the world; it is through equity that we have such concepts as transaction set-off, subrogation, the non-possessory lien and the greater part of restitutionary proprietary rights. So it is a little ungrateful to seek to accept all the benefits of equity without assuming some of the responsibilities it imposes in return. Moreover, as Sir Peter Millett has pointed out in his recent Chancery Bar association lecture[21]:

" . . . there is the growing complexity and professionalism of commercial life which have accompanied the change from an

---

[19] *M'Alister (or Donoghue) v. Stevenson* [1932] 1 A.C. 562 at 580.
[20] Kaplow, *loc. cit.*, at p. 577.
[21] *Equity's Place in the Law of Commerce.* This lecture has not yet been published and I am indebted to Sir Peter for supplying me with a copy of his text and for his permission to quote from it.

industrial to a service economy and the growth of the financial services industry. Much commerce today is based on trust; on each side of a commercial arms' length transaction there are likely to be relationships of trust and confidence. As a result, the modern fiduciary is usually a professional . . . Principles of equity designed to mitigate the severity of its rules as they bore on the well-meaning amateur are incongruous when applied to the paid professional."

We have only to look at the scandals that have occurred in the conduct of business at Lloyd's, the hardship and distress caused by the Maxwell affair, the huge litigation resulting from the collapse of the BCCI group of companies, and the misselling of personal pensions—all of these promoted by greed or the lure of extravagant commissions and bonuses—to realise that the morality of the market place has needed a degree of judicial leverage.

So equity plays an essential role in ensuring procedural fairness in contract bargaining and in requiring loyalty, good faith and the subordination of personal interest on the part of fiduciaries. That this encouragement of high standards of probity has distinct deterent and punitive elements should not cause us undue concern.[22] There are, however, certain boundaries to be observed if commercial life is not to be unduly disrupted.

First, the introduction of a concept of substantive unconscionability, in which the court takes it upon itself to declare a contract or its enforcement unfair, even where there has been no impropriety in the bargaining process and no conduct by the innocent party leading the other to believe that the innocent party will not assert his rights, would bring English law perilously close to adopting the medieval ecclesiastical principle of the just price and would, in my view, pose serious problems for the sanctity of commercial transactions. Again, great uncertainty would be engendered if the court, instead of adjudicating on the language of the contract governing default remedies, were to decide that, since performance was only a day or two late and the delay had not caused significant loss, the innocent party was not entitled to terminate the contract, or that a lender should allow a borrower a reasonable time to raise funds to

---

[22] See Cooter and Freedman, "The Fiduciary Relationship: Its Legal Character and Economic Consequences" 66 NYU L.Rev. 1045 (1991).

meet a demand before appointing a receiver. If protections of this kind need to be introduced into commercial transactions—and in the latter case an argument can be made for this—they should be introduced by a legislative rule, not by a judicial standard. Commercial people are used to tough bargains, often disguised in language of the most extraordinary prolixity.

We are, in my view, right to be cautious about adopting a general requirement of good faith in contracts, even though this is enshrined not only in the civil law but in the American Uniform Commercial Code and jurisprudence and has powerful supporters in England.[23] Very often one finds that recourse to the concept of good faith is used to bolster a conclusion that can easily be arrived at through the application of other, more specific, principles. Where this is not the case it can prove very difficult to give a definable content to the good faith standard and to predict the outcome of commercial disputes in which one party has sought to do no more than enforce the terms of a contract freely negotiated. For convincing evidence of this we need go no further than section 242 of the German Civil Code, which provides that: "The debtor is obliged to perform in accordance with the requirements of good faith, regard being had to ordinary usage." This innocuous-looking general clause, which has a contractual counterpart in section 157, has generated a mass of litigation to which more than 500 pages of detailed analysis have been devoted in the leading commentary on the BGB.[24] This is not to deny the benefits of a concept that the civilians have forged into a weapon of remarkable power and that also features strongly in the Unidroit *Principles of International Commercial Contracts*[25] and in the *Principles of European Contract Law*[26] prepared by the Commission on European Contract Law. But the stability of financial and commercial

---

[23] See, for example, Lord Steyn, "Contract Law: Fulfilling the Reasonable Expectations of Honest Men" (1997) 113 L.Q.R. 433 at 438–439. But Lord Steyn concludes that the introduction into English law of a general duty of good faith is not necessary, since courts can be relied on to respect the reasonable expectations of contracting parties through other means.

[24] Staudinger's *Kommentar zum Bürgerlichen Gesetzbuch* (13th ed., 1995). See also Markesinis, Lorenz and Dannerman, *The German Law of Obligations* (1997), Vol. I, which itself devotes an entire chapter of over 100 pages of case and commentary to the principle of good faith.

[25] Art. 1.7.

[26] Art. 1.106.

transactions is of especial importance for the world's leading financial centre; hence the preference of English law for party autonomy in the defining of substantive rights and for confinement of equitable relief to situations involving procedural unfairness.[27]

Secondly, it is important that the concept of a fiduciary, and of fiduciary obligations, should be confined to cases where one party justifiably reposes trust and confidence in the other and should not be extended to obligations in respect of which the parties' interests are essentially antagonistic. Lord Browne-Wilkinson has extra-judicially expressed concern over what he described as the "reach me down a fiduciary syndrome".[28]

Thirdly, the standard of conduct expected of a fiduciary, and the penalties imposed upon him, should not be set so high as to discourage the undertaking of fiduciary duties. Judicial thinking has moved on since the harsh decisions of the House of Lords in *Regal (Hastings) Ltd v. Gulliver*[29] and *Boardman v. Phipps*.[30] Today we are more ready to recognise that persons whose position as fiduciaries enables them to pursue a business opportunity should not necessarily be stripped of their profits where their beneficiaries or principals would not have been in a position to take up the opportunity if offered it. But the law of unjust enrichment continues to suffer from the lack of a limiting principle of remoteness of gains corresponding to rules of remotenesss in the law of contract and the law of tort. Where a fiduciary acts in breach of duty and through unusual skill and exertion reaps gains far beyond what might ordinarily have been expected to flow from his initial improper conduct, why is it nevertheless assumed that all the gains have resulted from that conduct, so that at best the defendant receives a generous allowance for his labours? Why does the law of unjust enrichment not possess some concept of legal causation to be found in

[27] It is possible that this will change when the courts have become accustomed to applying the good faith test embodied in the Unfair Terms in Consumer Contracts Regulations 1994. But the courts already apply a more protective standard to consumer contracts and may see no reason to extend a general concept of good faith to commercial dealings.

[28] "Equity in a Fast Changing World", presented to the Law Conference in Dunedin, New Zealand, in 1996.

[29] [1942] 1 All E.R. 378.

[30] [1967] 2 A.C. 96.

other branches of the law of obligations,[31] such as *novus actus interveniens*, proximate or direct cause, reasonable foreseeability or natural consequence?[32] There are now welcome signs that the courts are beginning to give greater thought to issues of causation in determining to what extent the defendant's gains are attributable to the wrong done to the plaintiff.[33]

Fourthly, equitable rules aimed at dishonest behaviour should not be artificially stretched to encompass what one might call constructive dishonesty; that is, acts which, though committed in good faith, were accompanied by a negligent failure to make inquiries that, if made, would have rendered those acts dishonest. In some cases the courts have been unable to resist the temptation to extend the concept of dishonesty in this way, particularly in relation to constructive trust claims based on knowing assistance in a breach of trust.[34] Fortunately, after much dithering, it now seems to be settled that only conduct involving moral turpitude will come within equity's net in this regard.[35]

Finally, equitable proprietary rights must not be extended so far as to undermine the rights of innocent third parties engaged in routine secured lending.

Has equity responded adequately to these commercial considerations? I believe that on the whole it has. It is not only common law judges who favour predictability. Distinguished equity lawyers have also emphasised the need to avoid uncertainty in commercial transactions.

"... wise judges have often warned against the wholesale importation into commercial law of equitable principles inconsistent with the

---

[31] On which see Hart and Honoré, *Causation in the Law* (2nd ed.), which, interestingly, focuses on harm caused by the defendant, not on benefit unjustly acquired.

[32] "For want of a nail the shoe was lost; for want of a shoe the horse was lost; for want of a horse the rider was lost; for want of a rider the battle was lost; for want of a battle the kingdom was lost; and all for the want of a horse-shoe nail!" But if I misappropriate my opponent's nail and win the battle, should I then be liable for the value of the kingdom?

[33] See, for example, *Warman International Ltd v. Dwyer* (1995) 182 C.L.R. 544 (a decision of the High Court of Australia), at 211–212.

[34] See, for example, *Baden v. Société Générale pour Favoriser le Développement de Commerce et de l'Industrie en France* [1983] B.C.L.C. 325; [1993] 1 W.L.R. 509; *Agip (Africa) Ltd v. Jackson* [1991] Ch. 547, *per* Fox L.J. at 567.

[35] *Royal Brunei Airlines Sdn Bhd v. Tan* [1995] 2 A.C. 378.

certainty and speed which are an essential requirement for the orderly conduct of business affairs."[36]

From time to time decisions have been made that cross what I would regard as the boundary of equitable intervention, but in the end a more controlled approach has usually prevailed. The one area in which, in my view, a wrong path has been taken is in relation to proprietary restitutionary rights, which have been extended to restitution through wrongs, thereby giving a plaintiff who has furnished no value and has suffered no detriment to his estate priority over trade creditors who have contributed to the defendant's assets. I have addressed this question elsewhere[37] and have returned to it[38] at the gathering in Cambridge in honour of that great pioneer of restitution law, Professor Gareth Jones, so I will not discuss it here.

(2) Tort liability for pure economic loss

Two issues are of relevance to the commercial world as regards tort liability for pure economic loss. The first is the concurrence of liability in contract and tort where a contracting party is guilty of negligence causing pure economic loss. Earlier authority against this concurrent liability, including a decision of the House of Lords, has now been consigned to oblivion.[39] I need say no more except to echo the view expressed many years ago by Professor Basil Markesinis that tort law is being forced to make up for the inadequacies of contract law.[40]

The second, and potentially much more dangerous, risk is that of being sued by a plaintiff with whom the defendant has had no dealings and of whose existence he may be wholly unaware, a risk particularly prevalent in relation to professional activity undertaken for and paid by a third party. We have seen propounded, in isolation or combination, a battery of tests to

---

[36] *Westdeutsche Landesbank Girozentrale v. Islington Borough Council* [1996] A.C. 669, *per* Lord Browne-Wilkinson at 704.

[37] See Roy Goode, "Property and Unjust Enrichment" in *Essays on the Law of Restitution* (ed. Andrew Burrows), Chap. 9.

[38] In a paper "Proprietary Restitutionary Claims", which is included in the volume of conference papers to be published in 1998 under the title *Restitution: Past, Present and Future* (ed. W.R. Cornish).

[39] *Henderson v. Merrett Syndicates Ltd* [1995] 2 A.C. 145.

[40] B.S. Markesinis, "An Expanding Tort Law—The Price of a Rigid Contract Law" (1987) 103 L.Q.R. 354.

determine whether a duty relationship exists: foreseeability, proximity and, more recently, public interest; and the shifts of judicial opinion this way and that have done little to promote the predictability upon which business depends. This is not a criticism of the judges; the problem of defining the limits of duty in this area is an intractable one, which does not admit of any single or simple formulation. But starting with the decision of the House of Lords in *Caparo*[41] there has been a welcome recognition of the need to avoid imposing liability on the professional for acts performed on behalf of a client which he had no reason to suppose would be communicated to or relied on by the plaintiff. The latest case is the decision of the High Court of Australia in *Esanda*,[42] in which a firm of accountants successfully defended a claim by investors who had relied on accounts audited, and allegedly negligently audited, by the defendants. In upholding an order dismissing a claim as disclosing no cause of action where the only plea was that the plaintiff's reliance on the audited accounts was reasonably foreseeable by the defendants, the High Court emphasised the need to show that the defendant ought reasonably to have known that the information supplied by him would be communicated to the plaintiff and would be likely to result in his entering into the kind of transaction he in fact entered into. Justices Gummow and McHugh warned of the costs of unpredictability and cautioned against too ready an assumption that insurance against open-ended liability was available and affordable or that the imposition of such liability was economically efficient or in the interests of creditors and investors.

I have emphasised the importance of predictability in commercial transactions. But predictability is not the same as certainty. Commercial life is itself inherently uncertain, and I have always thought that in litigation there is nothing like a healthy dose of uncertainty to promote a reasonable settlement. Even in the academic world—or perhaps particularly in the academic world—we thrive on uncertainty. The role of academics in general, and of textbook writers in particular, is to inject doubt where none existed before! And judges also reserve the right to change their minds even in commercial law. It was

[41] *Caparo Industries plc v. Dickman* [1990] 2 A.C. 605.
[42] *Esanda Finance Corp. Ltd v. Peat Marwick Hungerfords (Reg.)* (1997) 23 A.C.S.R. 71.

Baron Bramwell who, on being told that the line he was taking ran entirely counter to one of his own observations in an earlier case, replied that: "the matter does not appear to me now as it appears to have appeared to me then".[43] The judicial techniques for departing from a long line of established authority are highly developed. Every passage from an earlier judgment that appears to support the desired direction is carefully nurtured: a formulation of principle aimed at a very specific fact-situation is broadened into one of the most liberal compass; an *obiter dictum* is promoted to a statement of high authority. Conversely, prior authority that appears to stand in the way of progress is confined to its special facts (as witness the fate of the House of Lords decision in *Junior Books*[44]) or explained away as based on inappropriate concessions made by counsel in argument (as in the Court of Appeal decision in *Romalpa*[45]); or dismissed as yielding to "the dead hand of history" and "the temptation of elegance", as was said of cases ruling against concurrent liability in contract and tort for pure economic loss[46]; and if all else fails, an inconvenient leading case that has stood for over a hundred years can be wafted away on the ground that it was decided "perilously close to the long vacation".[47]

Form versus substance and function

Legal systems vary significantly in their approach to the role of the courts and to judicial reasoning. In some jurisdictions the emphasis is on formal reasoning—that is, on finding the

---

[43] *Andrews v. Styrap* (1872) 26 L.T. 704 at 706, in answer to a reference to a remark he had made in *Ellis v. Kelly* (1860) 6 H. & N. 222 at 226.

[44] *Junior Books Ltd v. Veitchi Co. Ltd* [1983] 1 A.C. 520, which attracted so much criticism that in the later decision of the Court of Appeal in *Simaan General Contracting Co. v. Pilkington Glass Ltd (No. 2)* [1988] Q.B. 758, Dillon L.J. was emboldened to say (at 784): "My own view of the *Junior Books* case is that the speeches of their Lordships have been the subject of so much analysis and discussion with differing explanations of the basis of the case that the case cannot now be regarded as a useful pointer to any development of the law, whatever Lord Roskill may have had in mind when he delivered his speech. Indeed I find it difficult to see that future citation from the *Junior Books* case can ever serve any useful purpose." This standpoint was vindicated by the later decision of the House of Lords in *D. & F. Estates Ltd v. Church Commissioners for England* [1989] A.C. 177.

[45] *Aluminium Industrie Vaassen BV v. Romalpa Aluminium Ltd* [1976] 1 W.L.R. 676.

[46] *Henderson v. Merrett Syndicates Ltd* [1995] 2 A.C. 145, *per* Lord Goff at 186.

[47] *Att.-Gen. of Hong Kong v. Reid* [1994] A.C. 324, *per* Lord Templeman at 334.

solution to a legal problem through the application of existing legal concepts and doctrine rather than by reference to economic, political or social considerations, and by characterising transactions according to the legal form in which they are cast rather than according to their economic substance and function. Elsewhere, the concern is to ensure that the law reflects relevant policy and what is perceived to be the reality of transactions. These fundamentally different approaches have been well described by my predecessor, Professor Patrick Atiyah, and his co-author Professor Robert Summers, in their trail-blazing work *Form and Substance in Anglo-American Law*. It is clear that, while both systems of law employ a mixture of the two forms approaches, the emphasis in English law is very much on formal reasoning and in American law on substantive reasoning. The latter is scarcely surprising, given the American constitutional framework and the fact that in a federal system the national law school has perforce to take a broad view of legal issues and to reflect in its teaching trends, or competing lines of legal thought, across the country rather than engaging in minute analyses of local law.

Form versus substance is what divides the legal from the accountancy profession. Both law and accounting convention require that accounts of a company reflect a true and fair view of its financial position, but the accounting view of truth is markedly different from that of the lawyer, the latter focusing on the legal form of a transaction, the latter on its economic substance. Of course, even in England form is not everything. The courts will not be bound by the label the parties attach to the transaction if it is a sham, in that it does not truly record what the parties have agreed, or if, though the agreement is genuine, the terms as whole show that its legal character is other than that designated by the parties. But where the transaction is not a sham the court will give it effect according to its terms and will not normally go outside the document to examine its economic substance or purpose except where it is so artificial as to possess no function apart from evasion of tax or other mandatory law.[48]

The battle of form versus substance rages particularly fiercely in relation to the characterisation of agreements creating

---

[48] See, for example, *Furniss v. Dawson* [1984] A.C. 474; *Ensign Tankers (Leasing) Ltd v. Stokes* [1992] 1 A.C. 655.

property rights, to which a somewhat more extended treatment will be given later in this lecture series.

Legal concepts versus legal policy

An aspect of the relative formalism of English law is that its approach to the solution of legal problems is, to a considerable degree, conceptual. We have concepts of ownership and of possession; we distinguish between property and obligation, between what I own and what I am owed; we have a concept of a fiduciary and of fiduciary obligations. Are concepts useful in commercial law? And how inviolate should they be?

It is interesting to see what has been happening in the United States. In many ways American lawyers are the most creative in the world in adapting their commercial law to changing commercial needs. We have only to look at Article 9 of the Uniform Commercial Code for its integrated approach to the treatment of security interests, and its jettisoning of outmoded distinctions between one security form and another, and, more recently, at the latest revision of Article 8 dealing with interests in securities, to see the power of the creative thought devoted to ensuring the continued relevance of commercial law to changing business needs. The great strength of leading American commercial lawyers lies in their perception of commercial law as essentially a tool for providing sensible solutions to typical problems. This has led modern American scholarship to be somewhat dismissive of the value of concepts and of conceptual reasoning, which are seen as obstacles to problem-solving. "We don't pay much attention to concepts these days", I was told many years ago by a leading American academic commercial lawyer. If that was truly his view, then I think it was profoundly mistaken, because legal ideas, like ideas in any other branch of knowledge, require an organising structure, and without concepts, principles and theories to guide them the courts would merely be reacting on a case-by-case basis to specific fact-situations, so that a ruling in one case would be no guide to the likely outcome of future disputes involving the same legal issue. That outstanding American jurist Karl Llewellyn, one of the founders of the realistic movement and a great commercial lawyer, surely put his finger on the point when he said:

> "Like rules, concepts are not to be eliminated; it cannot be done.
> Behaviour is too heterogeneous to be dealt with except after some

26

artificial ordering. The sense impressions which make up what we call observation are useless unless gathered into some arrangement. Nor can thought go on without categories."[49]

The renowned Lon Fuller wrote to similar effect:

"So many tirades have been launched against 'conceptualism' that one sometimes gains the impression that certain writers expect us to accomplish the impossible feat of reasoning without concepts. The trouble with the law does not lie in its use of concepts, nor even in its use of 'lump concepts'. The difficulty lies in part in the fact that we have sometimes put the 'lumps' in the wrong places, and in part in the fact that we have forgotten that the 'lumps' are the creations of our own minds."[50]

But concepts, a subject to which I will be returning, must be our servants, not our masters.[51] Llewellyn went on to point out that to classify is to disturb and that the process can be excused only in so far as it is necessary to the accomplishing of a purpose. If the purpose changes or the fact model from which the concept was derived disappears, then the received categories, however entrenched they might be, will need to be modified.[52] But this should done only with caution. Concepts and categories fulfil an important function in giving order and predictability. They will not provide justice in every case; that is not their function. The purpose is to ensure that in the typical case the law reaches a result which would commend itself to a fair-minded commercial community as being reasonable. What criteria should we adopt in deciding whether to modify or overthrow a concept? I would suggest the following. First, concepts are instruments of long-term value; they should therefore be disturbed as seldom as is compatible with the maintenance of their underlying purpose. Secondly, the more fundamental the concept the greater the care needed before it is amended or circumvented. Thirdly, before there is any interference with a concept the court should consider whether the effect of overriding it in a given type of case is to subordinate an important policy consideration to business expediency.[53]

[49] *Jurisprudence: Realism in Theory and Practice*, p. 27.
[50] *Legal Fictions*, p. 136.
[51] See further *post*, p. 70.
[52] Llewellyn, *op cit.*, pp. 27–28.
[53] See *post*, p. 70 and (1998) 114 L.Q.R. 8 at 11.

The role and influence of the law and economics movement

I would like to conclude this first lecture with some all-too-brief comments on a different aspect of the form versus substance debate, namely the role of economic theory in shaping commercial law. As the result of the pioneering work of such scholars as Calabresi, Coase and Posner (the last-named now a judge), we have come to see that economic theory has a role to play in legal policy. In particular, through its development of concepts of rational behaviour it provides the tools by which we can evaluate the economic efficiency of law and predict more accurately the outcomes of particular legal rules.

Now there is no doubt that in our contract and commercial law we do have regard to concepts of economic effiency—for example, in the so-called "duty" of the innocent party to mitigate loss resulting from the guilty party's breach of contract, the limits on the right to hold a contract open for performance, the rule that a decree of specific performance will usually be inappropriate where damages are an adequate remedy, the principle that risk should be imposed on the party best able to control it or to insure against it. But these principles and rules are often applied intuitively rather than on the basis of hard evidence. In certain areas of decision-making, such as competition policy, economics plays an important role in England, but it has been less influential on commercial law than in America, where the law and economics movement was born. This is due in some degree to the fact that the curricula for our university law courses are narrower, and less multi-disciplinary, than they are in North America or in continental Europe. That is a matter for regret. But there are other factors at work. We are not able, or at any rate not willing, to take law reform as seriously in this country as in the United States. We live in an era of short-termism, in which reforms not seen as having political appeal are unlikely to engage the attention of our political masters of whatever persuasion. Moreover, the preference for speedy results over sustained thought and investigation inhibits the work of even the most well-intentioned committee. So much of our legislation is based on anecdotal evidence and intuitive reasoning.

My own view is that economics has a greater potential role to play in legislation than in litigation. Economic theories result from the construction of sophisticated models designed to predict outcomes of legislative or judicial lawmaking. But it is necessary to remember that these are only models and that they rest on certain hypotheses which do not necessarily correspond with external facts. Even if we were prepared to accept that the rational being actually exists, we should have to admit that the complexities of business life are such that no group of economists, however eminent, could expect to take into account all the myriad factors that go to make up a rational decision. That is not a criticism of law and economics theory, for theories are by nature abstract, and it is precisely their generality that makes them useful. But theory needs to be tested against experience. Moreover, the law cannot be concerned solely with economic efficiency as the yardstick by which to measure the success of social goals. There are other factors at work—moral, political and psychological—which have to be considered. Finally, there is the practical problem of reaching decisions within a limited time and without disproportionate expense. It is this last problem in particular that limits the efficacy of economics as a tool for day-to-day litigation. Relatively few members of the judiciary on either side of the Atlantic can hope to emulate the interdisciplinary expertise of such judges as Learned Hand, Posner and Easterbrook. The admission of expert economic evidence in ordinary litigation would be likely to lead to protracted trials and greatly increased expense. But what we can learn from at least an introductory study of law and economics is that intuition is a poor substitute for empirical evidence and that in seeking to move the law in a particular direction we should not be too ready to make assumptions that, for example, insurance is available and affordable or that the imposition of a liability will induce or discourage desirable or undesirable behaviour.

Let me conclude with a quotation from the playwright Thomas Middleton, who anticipated Professor Ronald Coase by some 400 years in linking law and economics:

"The wretch, that lov'd before his food his strife,
This punishment falls even with his life,
His pleasure was vexation, all his bliss
The torment of another;
Their hurt his health, their starred hopes his store;
Who so loves law dies either mad or poor."[54]

---

[54] *The Phoenix*, Act IV, Scene I.

2. Contracts and Markets: The Challenges Confronting Public and Private Law

I CONTRACTS AND MARKETS IN PRIVATE LAW

Contract as the foundation of commercial law

At the heart of commercial law is the law of contract, with its central doctrines of freedom of contract and *pacta sunt servanda*: contracts are to be observed. It is impossible to overestimate the importance of freedom of contract in the development of English commercial law. It has facilitated the creation of financial and commodities markets which are among the most flexible and efficient in the world; it has also enabled English law to provide a regime for the creation and enforcement of security interests which is unrivalled for its informality and its willingness to allow the parties to define their own rights and remedies and to organise their relationships in whatever way they consider best suited to their needs. Further, it has instilled in traders from this country and abroad a sense of stability and predictability that is vital to commerce. This *laissez-faire* approach, which had been anticipated a century before by the founder of English commercial law, Lord Mansfield, led to the courts moving from an approach in which everything had to be justified by precedent or evidence of mercantile usage to one in which the role of the courts was seen as enforcing parties' bargains so long as they did not cross the line between acceptable and unacceptable behaviour.

Laissez-faire proved particularly accommodating to the recognition of trade usage, the reasonable and consistently applied usages and practices of merchants, which in the Middle Ages was of such importance that by statute the old law merchant was given precedence over the common law itself in disputes tried in the courts of the fairs and the staple,[1] and which to this day remains an important source of rights and obligations.

Nowadays it has become fashionable to downgrade contract and even to speak of its decline and fall. I have to say that this is not a world I recognise. It is true that the domain of contract law shrinks with the expansion of state trading and nationalisation, and that this leads to a consequent reduction of private law in favour of public law, as observed Professor Patrick Atiyah in his magisterial work *The Rise and Fall of Freedom of Contract*[2]; but if the wheel had then come full circle it is now on the move again, with privatisation and a restoration of the boundaries of contract law, a world-wide phenomenon. Contract is flourishing, and with remarkably few constraints outside the fields of competition, financial services and consumer protection. The essence of a market economy is competition and party autonomy. In such an economy the market is king. But, as we shall see, the freedom of the market is not readily reconcilable with the integrity of the market. The effecting of such a reconciliation is, perhaps, the greatest challenge confronting modern commercial law.

The strengths and weaknesses of English contract law

As I have said, English contract law attaches a high degree of importance to party autonomy. This has several beneficial effects. The parties can feel that they are in large measure the masters of their destiny; and the equally liberal regime governing assignments of contract rights and the creation of security and quasi-security interests enables them to set up almost any pattern of relationships they choose in order to carry out their legitimate business objectives. Finally, the law's benign approach to freedom of contract makes it much easier to predict the outcome of disputes than would be possible in a more paternalistic regime.

It would be tempting, then, to conclude that English contract law does not require any significant improvement. But I believe we cannot afford such complacency. The truth is that our contract law has not kept pace with legal thought and developments in other major jurisdictions. Its rules are unduly rigid, its

[1] Statute of the Staple, 27 Edw. III, stat. 2 (1353), cc. 5, 6, 8 and 21.
[2] At p. 719.

range of remedies is seriously deficient and it does not adequately distinguish discrete transactions from continuing, relational contracts. The adequacy of contract law can best be tested by asking the question: does it accommodate legitimate business expectations? To this one can give at best a qualified affirmative. Let me seek to make good this assertion with further and better particulars. I will refrain from comment about the doctrines of privity and consideration: both have been extensively canvassed in a number of different fora, and the Law Commission has recommended that third-party beneficiaries be given a right to enforce contracts made for their benefit.[3] But there are other causes for concern. Time allows me to mention only some of the more important of these.

(1) Agreements to negotiate

It is quite common for parties to enter into an agreement to negotiate. Civil law jurisdictions have no difficulty in recognising such an agreement as legally binding. It does not, of course, commit the parties to reach agreement; it *is* intended to commit them to making a bona fide effort to do so. Yet for some reason we find ourselves unable to give legal effect to such a commitment. Because the outcome of an agreement to negotiate it is indeterminate, we regard the agreement itself as void for uncertainty,[4] which is surely a *non sequitur*. It is time we brought ourselves into line on this issue with other European countries, whose courts find no great difficulty in giving content to an agreement to negotiate.

(2) Suspension of performance

Where a party to a contract commits a repudiatory breach it is well established that the other party has a choice: he may terminate the contract, thereby putting an end to the duties of future performance on both sides, or he can affirm it, in which case he must proceed with his own performance. The one thing he cannot do is to suspend performance until the guilty party signifies that he is now ready and able to perform.[5] This is truly

---

[3] *Privity of Contract: Contracts for the Benefit of Third Parties* (Law Com. No. 242, 1996).

[4] *Walford v. Miles* [1992] 2 A.C. 128, *per* Lord Ackner at 136.

[5] *Fercometal SARL v. Mediterranean Shipping Co. SA (The Simona)* [1989] A.C. 788.

astonishing. The remedy of suspension is available where the parties have expressly or impliedly agreed that performance and counter-performance of particular obligations are to be concurrent, as in the case of delivery and payment under a contract of sale of goods[6]; yet repudiation of the contract as a whole does not give the innocent party the same right; he is forced to choose between termination and continuance of his own performance.[7] This principle appears to apply both to an anticipatory breach and to a repudiation after the time for performance has arrived. In reference to the former situation the principle was succinctly expressed by Lord Ackner in the following terms:

"Where A wrongfully repudiates his contractual obligations in anticipation of the time for their performance, he presents the innocent party with two choices. He may either affirm the contract by treating it as still in force or he may treat it as finally and conclusively discharged. There is no third choice, as a sort of *via media*, to affirm the contract and yet to be absolved from tendering further performance unless and until A gives reasonable notice that he is once again able and willing to perform. Such a choice would negate the contract being kept alive for the benefit of *both* parties and would deny the party who unsuccessfully sought to rescind the right to take advantage of any supervening circumstance which would justify him in declining to complete."[8]

This principle is treated in our textbooks as equally applicable to a repudiatory breach committed after the time for performance has arrived.[9] There is no doubt that it is well established in English law. But why should the innocent party be faced with such a stark choice? Why should he not be able to say to the

---

[6] Sale of Goods Act 1979, s.28.

[7] A little leeway is indicated by the decision in *Yukong Line Ltd of Korea v. Rendsburg Investments Corp. of Liberia* [1996] 2 Lloyd's Rep. 604, where Moore-Bick J. held that a protest by the innocent party at the guilty party's repudiation and an invitation to the guilty party to withdraw its repudiation and confirm its willingness to perform did not amount to an affirmation of the contract by the innocent party. But in view of the decision in *Fercometal* (above, n. 5) it would seem that such a position can be held for only a short time and that if the guilty party were to persist in its repudiation the innocent party would have to decide whether to accept it or to affirm.

[8] *Fercometal* (above, n. 5), at 805.

[9] See, for example, *Chitty on Contracts* (27th ed.), para. 24–009; G.H. Treitel, *Law of Contract* (9th ed.), p. 757.

guilty party: "I will give you the opportunity to recant; until you do I will suspend performance"? The same applies to a defective tender of performance. I have argued elsewhere[10] that in this situation the affirmation–termination dichotomy is inadequate and that in a contract for the sale of goods, for example, it would exclude what is by far the most common choice of a buyer to whom non-conforming goods are tendered, namely to reject the goods while asking that they be repaired or replaced.

English law appears committed to the strange position that non-performance of even a minor obligation entitles the innocent party to suspend performance of a correlative obligation (that is, one which is to be performed at the same time as, and in exchange for, the first party's performance), whereas he has no right to suspend performance where the other party repudiates the entire contract. By contrast, suspension of performance is a well-recognised right in American contract law[11] and is enshrined in the civil law in the *exceptio non adimpleti contractus*. Surely we in England should now adopt the same approach.

(3) *Anticipatory breach and assurance of future performance*

Where, before a party's performance has become due, a party renounces his contractual obligations or disables himself from performing at the due date, the other party can elect to treat the contract as at end. But this well-established doctrine of anticipatory breach does not appear to cover the case where a party's conduct or circumstances merely gives rise to legitimate doubt as to whether he will be able to perform, for example, by his saying: "We've had a lot of industrial trouble lately; but don't worry—I'm 90 per cent sure that this will be settled and we'll get your goods to you on time." In such a case, American law, as reflected in the Uniform Commercial Code,[12] allows the potentially affected party to ask for reasonable assurance of performance, failing which he can treat the contract as at an end; and a similar rule is embodied in the Unidroit *Principles of International Commercial Contracts*,[13] the *Principles of European Contract Law*[14] prepared by the Commission on European Con-

---

[10] *Commercial Law* (2nd ed.), p. 132.

[11] See E. Allan Farnsworth, *Farnsworth on Contracts*, §§8.15, 8.16, 8.22, and 1996 Supplement.

[12] s.2.609.

[13] Art. 7.3.4.

[14] Art. 3.105.

tract Law, and, as regards financial insecurity, section 321 of the German Civil Code. We should follow their example.

(4) The doctrine of frustration

English law is very reluctant to recognise change of circumstances as a ground for relieving parties of their contractual obligations. The starting point is that the parties can always provide in their contract for events which substantially alter the economic equilibrium of the contract, and if they choose not to do so that is their affair: they have made their bed, they must lie in it. English law has not yet adopted the softer, American version of frustration covering cases where performance has become impracticable.[15] Only in extreme circumstances, such as physical destruction of the subject-matter of the contract, supervening illegality or disappearance of the whole substratum of the contract, will the law give relief. And in these cases the relief takes the form of automatic termination of the contract by force of law. The all-or-nothing nature of this doctrine of frustration, as it is termed, is striking. English law knows no halfway house between full enforceability and automatic termination by force of law. Modification of a contract through change of circumstances falling short of frustration is not a remedy to be found in the medicine chest of our contract law. This reflects the long-established principle that it is not for the courts to remake the parties' bargains.

Yet the remedy of contract modification would have alleviated the hardship caused to the sellers in the *Noblee Thorn* case,[16] who as the result of the closure of the Suez Canal in November 1956 faced having to ship the goods from Port Sudan to Hamburg via the Cape of Good Hope, increasing the journey from 4,836 miles to 11,137 miles and doubling the freight. All the tribunals involved in the case, from the original umpire up to the House of Lords, held that the required performance was not fundamentally different from that originally envisaged, and the sellers were liable in damages for their failure to perform.

If this all-or-nothing approach causes hardship in the case of discrete contracts, it is potentially still more severe as regards

[15] See *Restatement (Second) of Contracts*, §261; Uniform Commercial Code, s.2–615 (for contracts of sale); Farnsworth, *op. cit.*, §9.6.
[16] *Tsakiroglou & Co. Ltd v Noblee Thorn GmbH* [1962] A.C. 93.

the continuing long-term contract, which by its nature depends for its efficacy as much on relationships as on performance and which cannot be expected to provide for the infinite variety of changes that may occur over the lifetime of the contract. For these contracts in particular the all-or-nothing effect of the doctrine of frustration is too blunt an instrument. Hence the Unidroit *Principles of International Commercial Contracts* provide that where the occurrence of events fundamentally alters the equilibrium of the contract the disadvantaged party is entitled to request renegotiations, and failing agreement within a reasonable time the court may terminate the contract at a date and on terms to be fixed, or adapt the contract with a view to restoring its equilibrium.[17] Similar provisions are contained in the *Principles of European Contract Law*, prepared by the Commission on European Contract Law.[18] Is there a judicial route to this result? It seems to me that this is a legitimate case for invoking a doctrine of substantive unconscionability. It would be inequitable for a party to seek to hold the other to the terms of the original bargain in the light of changed circumstances, and reasonable that the court should offer him the choice of accepting modification of the contract or having it terminated by the court. German courts have for many years admitted such a remedy, relying either on the requirement of good faith in section 242 of the German Civil Code or on the judicially applied principle of *Wegfall der Geschäftsgrundlage* (collapse of the basis of the transaction) first enunciated by Professor Paul Oertmann; whilst in France the Conseil d'État long ago developed the theory of *imprévision* to provide the remedy of contract adaptation for public law contracts that have become unduly burdensome by reason of unforeseeable circumstances.

The continuing inadequacies of contract law stem from the fact that since the unfortunate abandonment of the Law Commission's attempted codification of the law of contract[19] we have

---

[17] Arts 6.2.2–6.2.3.
[18] Art. 6.111.
[19] The draft Contract Code, prepared on behalf of the English and Scottish Law Commissions by Harvey McGregor, was an outstanding one-man achievement. In 1972, however, the Scottish Law Commission withdrew from the project, which was then abandoned, and McGregor's Code was never published by the Commissions. But in 1993 the phoenix arose from the ashes with the publication of the full text and commentary by Giuffré Editore and Sweet

not in this country made any systematic attempt to re-examine our contract law as a whole. It is time for a *renvoi* to that exercise in the light of modern scholarship and legal developments elsewhere.

The role of the market

I have referred to the central role of contract in commercial law. Yet if commercial law had rested simply on a series of disconnected bilateral contracts it would have remained a puny child indeed. What gave it force was the organised market, the physical meeting place—and, in more recent times, the electronic communication network—administered by organisations of merchants or bankers, with its rules of membership, its facilities for the introduction of sellers to buyers and lenders to borrowers, its development of standard contracts which could themselves be traded on the market isolated, as it were, from the underlying commodities, its code of conduct for the transaction of business and its systems for the clearing and settlement of transactions and for currency exchanges. It is through the rules and practices of the organised market, and from the market's power and competitive thrust, that the fullest play can be given to the creative genius of the merchant and his lawyer. The rules and usages of the market bind the participants to common standards and practices. They bolt a mass of bilateral contracts onto a framework of standard terms, each participant undertaking to the others to observe the rules of the market.

Physical markets, in the dual sense of subject-matter (goods and money) and face-to-face at meeting places, have existed from the earliest days of civilisation. In England special protection was given to the purchaser of goods in market overt—an open, legally constituted market. The purchaser acquired a good title, even if buying from a thief, so long as he bought in good faith between the hours of sunrise and sunset and, in the case of purchase in a shop within the City of London, from the front, not the rear, of the shop.[20] Market overt was abolished in 1994,

& Maxwell under the auspices of the University of Pavia. Though now overtaken by the contract codes produced by Unidroit and the Commission on European Contract Law, the McGregor Code remains an invaluable source and, indeed, has been taken up by the Academy of European Private Lawyers in its own work on a European contract code.

[20] With multiple entrances to modern shops it is sometimes far from easy to distinguish the front from the rear!

frustrating my long-standing ambition to undertake a complete survey of markets overt in England and Wales!

Modern markets are altogether more specialised and sophisticated. They are no longer confined to physical objects or to open outcry; they can be organised around any mode of networked communication and virtually any kind of asset, tangible or intangible. But the key characteristics remain the same: an organisational structure to match sellers to buyers and lenders to borrowers; the establishment of systems for currency exchange and for the clearing and settlement of transactions; the standardisation of contracts, developed to the point where contracts themselves, detached from the underlying goods or other objects, can be traded on the market; and the regulation of each market in the interests of the participants and, in theory at least, of the public.

Two developments have powered the modern market. The first is securitisation, the commodification of contract rights, in which non-tradable debt receivables are converted into securities issued in unitised form on the market or are used as security for issues of bonds and loan notes, credit enhancement being given by means of guarantees and standby letters of credit. The effect of securitisation is disintermediation, the shifting of loan assets from banks to the financial markets. As was noted in the Wallace Report on Financial Systems in Australia: "The evolution of financial systems has been characterised by a continuing struggle between financial intermediaries and financial markets."[21] The second development is the growth of abstract undertakings, engagements which finance or hedge underlying trade transactions but are conceptually independent of them or which alternatively are concluded purely by way of speculation and are unrelated to any underlying transaction. This principle of abstraction is not new. The great French historian Fernand Braudel, writing of the Amsterdam Stock Exchange at the beginning of the seventeenth century, observed that:

> ". . . speculation on the Amsterdam Stock Exchange had resulted in a degree of sophistication and abstraction which made it for many years a very special trading centre of Europe, a place where people would not contract simply to buy and sell shares, speculating on

[21] *Financial Systems Inquiry Final Report*, March 1997, p. 159.

their possible rise or fall, but where one could by means of various ingenious combinations speculate without having any money or shares at all."[22]

Markets and clearing systems bring together a large number of players, and the amounts committed or invested in a single day's trading are potentially enormous. It is therefore scarcely surprising that our courts, versed as they are in commercial dealings, make every effort to uphold reasonable market practice and measures taken to preserve and protect the integrity of the market. Courts are reluctant to reach conclusions which will put at risk a large volume of transactions or undermine market regulation. Two examples will suffice. In *United Dominions Trust Ltd v. Kirkwood*[23] the plaintiffs, a large finance house, brought proceedings on certain bills of exchange. The defence was that the plaintiffs were unlicensed moneylenders and the transactions were therefore unenforceable, to which the plaintiffs made reply that they were bankers and thus exempt from the Moneylenders Acts. At risk, if this contention were right, was the recovery of loans to the value of several million pounds. The Court of Appeal, having held unanimously that the evidence did not show that the plaintiff's conduct of their business possessed the usual characteristics of banking, nevertheless divided on the result. Lord Denning, after finding that none of the main activities of the plaintiffs sufficed to establish them as bankers, went on to invoke the spirit of Lord Mansfield and to say that on the evidence they were treated by the banking community as bankers and what their claim to banking status lacked in terms of legal definition could be made good by reputation.

"Reputation may exclude a person from being a banker, so also it may make him one. Our commercial law has been founded on the opinion of merchants . . . When merchants have established a course of business which is running smoothly and well with no inconvenience or injustice, it is not for the judges to put a spoke in the wheel and bring it to a halt. Even if someone is able to point to a flaw, the courts should not seize on it so as to invalidate past transactions or produce confusion."[24]

[22] *Civilisation and Capitalism*, Vol. 2, *The Wheels of Commerce* (trans. Sîan Reynolds (1982)), p. 101.
[23] [1966] 2 Q.B. 431.
[24] *ibid.*, at 454–455.

Lord Justice Diplock would have none of this. Reputation could not in his view make people into bankers whose business was not that of banking. However, the court was entitled to infer from the evidence that the plaintiffs' reputation as bankers was well founded. So for a different reason he agreed with the conclusion of the Master of the Rolls. The third member of the court, Lord Justice Harman, felt reluctantly compelled to the conclusion that the plaintiffs were unregistered moneylenders.

Still more striking was the decision in *Shearson Lehmann*,[25] one of the many actions arising from the collapse of the International Tin Council. Many of you will recall the facts of this extraordinary affair. The ITC was set up by a group of 23 sovereign states and the EEC to provide a mechanism to stabilise the tin market. A buffer stock manager was appointed with a fund of money to buy tin where the market was unduly depressed and a quantity of tin to sell where prices were too high. Tin prices fell sharply, so the manager used funds to buy tin. Despite successive purchases on his part the price of tin continued to fall. He used up all the ITC's funds, borrowed from the banks and used up all their money as well, but still the price of tin relentlessly fell. The ITC then ceased trading and declared a default on its loans. The sovereign states and the EEC declined to accept responsibility. The ITC was an international organisation possessing a distinct juristic personality and they had no responsibility for its debts. That was the background.

My concern is not with the attempts made to recover the loans but with the steps taken by the London Metal Exchange to restore order in the market. Its measures could fairly be described as draconian. By a new rule, Rule M, all sale contracts still open on cessation of trading by the ITC were directed to be closed out by repurchase contracts at a settlement price fixed by the LME and differences paid by the date specified by the Exchange. Thus contracts freely concluded on the market were retrospectively negated. It is not surprising that Rule M and the action of the LME in promulgating it were challenged. The plaintiffs claimed damages for breach of contract resulting from their counterparty's refusal to perform in reliance on Rule M. That Rule and the powers exercised under it were attacked on a great many grounds covering both private and public law. All

---

[25] *Shearson Lehman Hutton Inc. v. Maclaine Watson & Co. Ltd* [1989] 2 Lloyd's Rep. 570.

of them failed. Webster J. held that Rule M and associated measures taken pursuant to the powers it conferred were protected by the agreement of the members to be bound by rules promulgated by the Exchange and by the overriding need to preserve the stability of the market, and that non-members (including the plaintiff) were bound by separate agreements, though only to rules in force at the time the agreements had been concluded. In the case of the plaintiff this did not include Rule M, so the plaintiff was entitled to damages. It is clear that but for this fact the defence would have succeeded. What the case demonstrates is the power of the market to pull itself up by its own legal bootstraps and the pressure on courts to avoid decisions that would threaten the orderly continuance of the market.

This is not to say that market transactions are off-limits to the courts. The common law is ready with remedies in tort for deceit and negligent misstatements, whilst equity provides the right of rescission for misrepresentation, holds fiduciaries to a high standard of conduct and provides an aggrieved party with both personal and proprietary remedies for unjust enrichment. These duties and remedies are buttressed by financial services legislation, which lays down or provides for detailed rules for the conduct of market operations, though it is not always clear to what extent these rules displace rather than supplement fiduciary obligations in equity.[26] And this brings me by a natural progression to the role of public law in commerce.

II CONTRACTS AND MARKETS IN PUBLIC LAW

Public law can affect markets and market contracts in at least four different ways. First, the decisions of regulatory authorities and other bodies, public or private, whose activities involve the exercise of public functions, may be challenged by way of judicial review on the ground of illegality, irrationality or procedural impropriety.[27] So where, as the result of a decision

---

[26] See the Law Commission's Consultation Paper No. 124, *Fiduciary Duties and Regulatory Rules* (1992).

[27] *Council of Civil Service Unions v. Minister for the Civil Service* [1985] A.C. 374, *per* Lord Diplock at 410.

objectionable on one of these grounds, a company is denied a statutory franchise or is excluded from or rendered liable to suspension from an exchange or has its authorisation to carry on a particular type of business revoked or refused, the decision may be quashed. There is now a substantial body of law dealing with what has become known as commercial judicial review.[28] Secondly, commercial interests are protected by European law in a number of ways. For example, European Community law confers rights to free movement of capital, the right of establishment and entitlement to review of a decision refusing or revoking a Stock Exchange listing; and the European Court of Justice has recently held that the refusal of Her Majesty's Treasury to authorise debits to the account of the National Bank of Yugoslavia in London for the price of medical supplies to Serbia and Montenegro for exports not made from the United Kingdom was contrary to the common commercial policy of the European Community provided in Article 113 of the E.C. Treaty.[29] What may be rather less well known is that the European Convention on Human Rights, which the government intends to incorporate into the law of this country, protects legal as well as natural persons and thus creates what are sometimes called commercial human rights. These include the protection of property from confiscation without compensation, the enjoyment of rights without discrimination on the ground of nationality, and freedom of expression in being able to disseminate information without interference from public authorities.[30] Thirdly, the conduct of markets may be regulated by statute or under statutory powers, as in the case of markets in financial services, or may be affected by rules of law such as restrictions on netting and set-off in insolvency. Dealings on or with reference to the rules of an organised financial market are primarily what distinguish regulated investment from unregulated trade. Fourthly, public law may come into conflict with private rights where a transaction is impeached as having been entered into by a public body or local authority outside its statutory powers. I shall say nothing further about the first two of these, and focus on the others.

[28] See, for example, *R. v. LAUTRO, ex p. Ross* [1993] Q.B. 17; *R. v. Panel on Takeovers and Mergers, ex p. Datafin* [1987] Q.B. 815.

[29] Case C–124/95 *R. v. H.M. Treasury* [1997] E.C.R. I–114; [1997] 3 W.L.R. 239.

[30] See Peter Duffy, "The Protection of Commercial Interests under the European Convention on Human Rights" in *Making Commercial Law* (ed. Ross Cranston), Chap. 23.

Market regulation

The regulation of markets is of long standing in English law. Much of this has taken the form of self-regulation. Organised markets have invariably found it necessary to devise rules for the conduct of the market, though these usually had more to do with the rights and duties of market members among themselves than with safeguards for outsiders, who were to a considerable degree dependent upon statutes or local ordinances. Among the earliest of these were statutes designed for the protection of public health and prohibiting, for example, the sale of rotten food and adulterated beer. At a later stage came legislation which reinforced common law rules designed to ensure that an adequate supply of products was available on the market at a fair price. So it became an offence to engage in ingrossing (buying goods in bulk with a view to profiteering), forestalling (buying goods before they reached the market or inducing a prospective seller not to bring his goods to the market), regrating (buying goods and selling them in the same or a neighbouring market) or any other form of price manipulation.

Of the modern types of market regulation, by far the most wide-ranging and complex are those contained in the financial services legislation and in rules made by the Securities and Investments Board and self-regulating organisations. To these must be added the complex requirements imposed by the London Stock Exchange relating to public issues, takeover procedures and the like. It is interesting that the statutory provisions do not seem to be aimed at market manipulation as such but only at the creation of a false market through failure to disclose relevant information or through conduct that engenders a false or misleading impression of the market and is engaged in for that purpose.[31] Thus attempts to corner the market do not, as such, appear to be prohibited, nor do sales made with the aim of inducing a fall in the market so as to allow opportunities to buy back at a reduced price or purchases made in order to drive up the market price with a view to reselling at a profit.

Why regulation?

Why should the law regulate markets at all? The question is worth asking because there is widespread misunderstanding in

[31] Financial Services Act 1986, s.47(1), (2).

the public mind about the role of regulation and regulators. Regulation is designed to fulfil a number of distinct but related functions.[32] One is to address potential imperfections in the market through rules as to fair and free competition, transparency of dealings, disclosure of relevant information, equality of treatment among market participants and the prohibition of acts that create a false market, for example by share support operations. All such rules have as their goal protection of the integrity of the market. With these go rules governing admission to the market and intended to ensure that market participants have the necessary competence, integrity and financial standing. A second objective is maintenance of the stability of the market through protective measures intended to avoid violent fluctuations leading to a loss of confidence, which could feed on itself to the point of endangering the very existence of the market. Such importance is attached to market stability that stabilisation procedures such as over-allotment and under-allotment of an initial issue are given special exemption from rules relating to market manipulation. The third, and most important of all, is the control of risk. Here it is necessary to distinguish risk of an isolated failure of an individual player from systemic risk—that is, the risk that major failures of one or more participants will undermine the market as a whole.

It is widely assumed that the task of public regulation is to prevent business failures and that if, say, a bank or major company becomes insolvent this conclusively demonstrates that the regulatory system in general and the regulator in particular were at fault. It is important that this assumption, which predicates that investment should somehow be altogether free of credit risk, should be vigorously dispelled, for if it were well founded there would be no incentive for investors to act prudently in their own interests. The Wallace Report, dealing with financial services in Australia, addressed the point in admirably trenchant terms:

"Risk is an intrinsic feature of financial products, and a major role of financial markets is to manage, allocate and price risk. The ultimate source of risk is commercial, and constitutes the inherent uncertainty facing all economic activities. This risk can never be eliminated, but it

[32] As regards banking regulation, see Ross Cranston, *Principles of Banking Law* (1997), Chap. 3.

can usually be allocated through markets to those who are willing to bear it for appropriate reward. Thus, it is not the role of regulation to eliminate financial risk wherever it arises. To do so would destroy the vital risk-management role of financial markets with highly adverse consequences for economic activity. It is therefore necessary to circumscribe the application of financial safety regulation. This is all the more so because financial safety regulation can induce 'moral hazard' by encouraging the risky behaviour it is seeking to deter."[33]

I would go further still and challenge the ingrained belief in our society that the insolvency of an enterprise denotes a failure of regulation and of our system of commerce. Business failure can be broadly attributed to one or more of three causes: fraud, mismanagement and bad luck. Fraud is usually exceptional and detectable, sooner or later, but there is no way of preventing it. Mismanagement is simply a manifestation of inherent human frailty, though we could no doubt reduce the risk of it by providing management training for company directors. Bad luck can come in a variety of forms: loss of a market, failure of a major debtor, or yet another blockade by French lorry drivers. No amount of regulation can prevent, or even forecast, any of these things. But more importantly, business failure should be seen as a necessary consequence of a market-oriented society. Entrepreneurial activity involves the taking of risks. The only way of avoiding risk is by not undertaking any business activity whatsoever. If, therefore, we wish to encourage enterprise we must accept the risk of insolvency as part of the price to be paid; indeed, the insolvency process is a necessary mechanism for promoting the stability and efficiency of the market by eliminating inefficient and badly run enterprises.

Systemic risk is quite another matter. The collapse of an entire market through the domino effect of failure of a major player is something that no government can regard as acceptable. The reason why banks are so closely regulated is not simply that they accept deposits from the public but that their day-to-day exposure in their relations with other banks is potentially enormous, and in a multilateral netting system the failure of a major bank to meet its obligations could create huge difficulties for other participants, as well as engendering a widespread loss of confidence. So while the problem of moral hazard precludes

[33] *Financial Services Inquiry Final Report*, p. 19.

the adoption of any principle that bank depositors must be protected at all costs, the risk of a failure to the system as a whole means, in practice, that support has to be found for banks in difficulty,[34] typically through the Bank of England or by means of acquisition by another bank, as happened with Barings. Thus we find a battery of measures designed to reduce systemic risk: prudential supervision, capital adequacy requirements, the introduction of real-time gross settlement for large payments, the enactment of legislation designed to give multilateral netting immunity from attack under insolvency law, and clearing house rules which substitute the clearing house as debtor and creditor in market operations, the clearing house's position being protected by the obligations of its members and its rules for margin deposits. European Union Directives and proposed Directives have played a prominent role in all but the last of these measures, and in an era of increasing volatility in the markets we can expect them to be kept under regular review.

The mode of regulation

Given the need for a measure of control over business activities and transactions, what form should this take? There are at least three sets of alternatives to consider.

(1) *Regulation versus self-regulation*

The regime set up by the Financial Services Act had at its core the concept conveniently, if somewhat misleadingly, known as self-regulation—that is, control by members of the regulated categories themselves within a framework of statutory regulation. I never thought much of this idea. How can we expect members of the business or banking community to sit in judgment on their peers on practices in which they themselves engage? We have only to look at the scandalous misselling of pensions, from which leading life offices were huge beneficiaries, and at the shocking treatment of outside Names by certain Lloyd's underwriting agents that required litigation in order to force recognition of the magnitude of the problem and, in the end, an acceptable settlement, to realise that external controls are essential. So when my Pension Law Review Committee

---

[34] Cranston (*op. cit.*, n.32), pp. 96 *et seq.*

47

considered the shape of pensions regulation we eschewed the idea of self-regulation and recommended a statutory regulator. Hence the creation of the Occupational Pensions Regulatory Authority. Now the financial services regime is being moved in the same direction, with the abolition of the self-regulating organisations and the assumption of exclusive control by a so-called super-SIB, the Financial Services Authority.

Why does self-regulation not work? In my view, it is because it is expecting too much of human nature in the light of the overwhelming influence of competitive forces. For many years competition has been hailed as the great god; leave everything to market forces and good order and justice will prevail. Now I do not deny the several advantages of competition. By breaking down monopolies and closed shops it keeps organisations on their toes, encourages innovation, reduces prices and improves the quality of service. But all this is bought at a price which we are only now coming to appreciate. In a self-regulated market—which is not always readily distinguishable from an unregulated market—competition does not enhance ethical behaviour; on the contrary, it undermines it and intensifies the pursuit of self-interest at the expense of others. As Rudyard Kipling observed, by far the oldest law is the law of the jungle. When the ability to carry on a full range of banking services was limited to a relatively small number of banks recognised by the Bank of England, the conduct of banking business was no doubt conservative and lacking in innovation, but at least standards of ethical behaviour were on the whole observed and the Bank of England was able to exercise moral suasion without the need for any legislative powers whatsoever. But once we abandoned the concept of banking and opened up membership of the financial services industry, such control became less and less practicable. Newcomers entered the field with perceptions of banking as being a business rather than a profession. Their drive for a greater share of the market forced even the former aristocrats of banking to cut corners, to concern themselves less with ethical considerations than formerly and to move as financial conglomerates into areas of activity they knew nothing about. When large profits came in from the activities of a high-flying dealer, disbelief was suspended, rules of prudential supervision relaxed and huge losses suffered in consequence. Moreover, the ferocity of competition, and the fear of being left behind, meant that incompetence and unethical behaviour were not confined to back-street traders and financiers; it was the market leaders themselves who were among the worst offenders. So the very freedom upon which competition depends necessitates regulation, and I warmly welcome the new approach adopted by government. Of course, what I would call private law self-regulation, in the shape of rules governing the operational conduct of the market, will continue to play a useful role in reinforcing public law regulation. But it must be the province of statutory regulators to ensure the observance of statutory rules and standards and to enforce compliance.[35]

(2) *Rules versus discretions*

Cutting across the regulation/self-regulation divide is the issue of rules versus discretions. I have already discussed the high degree of importance attached by the commercial world to the predictability of decision-making.[36] This would seem to suggest a strong preference for rules over discretionary powers. Yet businessmen will argue with equal vehemence for the need to avoid rigidity and to have in place a scheme of regulation that is sufficiently flexible to accommodate changing needs and situations unforeseen by the regulations. Moreover, the complexities of commercial life are such that it is futile to seek rules to cover every conceivable situation. Well-meaning but misguided attempts to do so are the root cause of the complexity of much of our legislation. And the more detailed the rules, the more we impel the courts to a literal construction of them, for if, despite a profusion of language, no mention is made of the act or omission of which complaint is made, the assumption must be that it was not intended to be covered. Frederick of Prussia promulgated a code running to more than 19,000 sections and designed to cover all known and future legal problems. He was evidently surprised at the lack of enthusiasm for this gargantuan product! In any event, one thing is certain: that there remained an infinite number of situations for which even Frederick's code would not have made provision.

So if reliance on self-regulation was misplaced, I believe also that we have been going in the wrong direction in the style of

---

[35] For a detailed examination of the advantages and shortcomings of self-regulation, in which it is concluded that self-regulatory bodies are not ideally suited for the task of supervising market behaviour, see Brian Cheffins, *Company Law* (1997), Chap. 8.
[36] See *ante*, pp. 14 *et seq.*

our regulation and in our sanctions for market malpractice. Rule-making, particularly in relation to disclosure requirements, is now completely out of control. As to disclosure, I sometimes wonder whether those who formulate the rules appreciate that disclosure is effective only if confined to a strictly limited number of items; disclosure beyond this point becomes self-defeating, for the ordinary reader becomes confused or switches off altogether. What, for example, is the non-professional investor supposed to make of the information contained in an 80-page prospectus? Far better to give him or her two pages of essential facts and an indication that further information is available on request. More generally, if we have standards of business conduct, why try to cover in specific rules every kind of mischief, every type of required conduct, that the standards are intended to embrace? Fewer rules and more rigorously enforced standards are surely the solution. These can usefully be reinforced by codes of practice approved by the regulator.[37]

The task, therefore, is to balance the need for predictability against the countervailing need, which is of particular importance in commercial transactions, for a degree of flexibility which will accommodate new business products and practices. This balance is not easy to achieve.[38] If discretionary powers are too open-ended there is always the risk that their use will be determined by the personal predilections of the adjudicator. Moreover, both regulator and regulated perceive the importance of transparency and consistency in decision-making. Courts are particularly sensitive to this. No sooner does Parliament confer on the court a new discretionary power, unlimited in terms, than the judges themselves proceed to cut it down by formulating criteria for its exercise. Administrators likewise feel impelled to establish guidelines for themselves as their experience develops so as to facilitate the treatment of like cases in a like manner. Thus over time rules and discretionary standards tend

---

[37] Under s.124 of the Fair Trading Act 1973 the Director General of Fair Trading is placed under a duty to encourage relevant associations to prepare, and to disseminate to their members, codes of practice for guidance in safeguarding and promoting the interests of consumers in the United Kingdom.

[38] There is now a voluminous literature on this subject. See, in particular, Julia Black, *Rules and Regulations* (1997); Keith Hawkins (ed.), *The Uses of Discretion* (1992) and D.J. Galligan, *Discretionary Powers: A Legal Study of Official Discretion* (1986).

to converge.[39] Yet the power of the latter in the regulation of business practice is undeniably broader. The Bank of England has extensive powers under the Banking Act 1987 to refuse or revoke authorisation to carry on a deposit-taking business. Necessarily the exercise of this power depends heavily on the Bank's judgment of the integrity, competence and financial stability of the person seeking or holding authorisation. In the field of consumer law it is interesting to contrast the concept of unfairness to consumers in section 34(2) of the Fair Trading Act 1973 with the kind of misconduct the Director General of Fair Trading is required to take into account under section 25(2) of the Consumer Credit Act 1974 in deciding whether a person is fit to hold or continue to hold a licence to carry on a consumer credit business. Under the former provision a course of conduct can be regarded as unfair to consumers only where it consists of a criminal offence or a breach of duty under the civil law. Section 25(2), on the other hand, requires the Director to have regard to any evidence tending to show any one or more of five categories of misconduct, the last of which is that the person concerned has "engaged in any business practices appearing to the Director to be deceitful or oppressive, or otherwise unfair or improper *(whether unlawful or not)*".[40] This power is regularly used to induce consumer credit institutions to abandon business practices which, though lawful, are considered unfair,[41] and to do so even in relation to transactions entirely outside the scope of the Consumer Credit Act.[42]

---

[39] Indeed, they are almost invariably inseparable, for just as rules evolve for the exercise of discretion so also discretion is involved in the interpretation of rules. See Keith Hawkins, "The Use of Legal Discretion: Perspectives from Law and Social Science" in *The Abuses of Discretion* (ed. Hawkins) at pp. 35 *et seq.*

[40] Emphasis added. See generally Gordon Borrie, *The Development of Consumer Law and Policy—Bold Spirits and Timorous Souls* (the 1984 Hamlyn Lectures), Chap. IV, dicussing administrative regulation.

[41] For example, the making of "non-status" loans to consumers whose circumstances are known to be such that they will not be able to make repayment when this becomes due.

[42] For example, in relation to the use of the rule of 78 in computing rebates for early settlement in credit transactions involving credit above £15,000 and therefore not regulated by the Consumer Credit Act. For transactions within the Consumer Credit Act the regulator has no power to interfere, since use of the rule of 78 is prescribed by the Consumer Credit (Rebate on Early Settlement) Regulations 1983. So on this particular issue we have the paradox that the consumer is given greater protection for unregulated transactions than for those that are regulated by the Act.

If we are to avoid excessive rule-based prescription, it is necessary to have in place fairly wide-ranging discretionary powers to control market malpractice and to ensure as far as possible the competence and financial soundness of banking and securities institutions. But to mitigate the risk of arbitrary or unfair decisions it is essential to provide an administrative appeal system by which appeals can be heard by an individual or panel external to the regulator, the adherence to proper procedures being buttressed by the final recourse of judicial review. It is interesting to see the burgeoning use of the judicial review procedure by commercial concerns. This weapon can be expected to be used with growing frequency when we enact the European Convention on Human Rights and the business world becomes more aware than it appears to be at present of the safeguards which the Convention offers against arbitrary interference with fundamental freedoms.

(3)   *Civil penalties versus criminal sanctions*

It seems to me that criminalisation of improper activity is not the way to go. Criminal proceedings for major malpractice are almost invariably contested, they are oppressively lengthy and expensive and all too often fail on account of their complexity or problems of proof. Far better to introduce a system of civil penalties, such as those imposed by the American Securities and Exchange Commission, which can be accepted without admission of guilt but which send the necessary signal to the market. And where prosecutions are brought, why not bring them for the smaller infraction, to which there is usually no defence, such as the failure to file accounts? This, too, sends a signal to the market and at vastly reduced cost.

Legal risk

So far, I have discussed measures for the protection of the public against the risk of insolvency or improper trading. But business risk and behavioural risk do not cover the whole field; markets are also acutely concerned over legal risk, the risk that market transactions or operations, even where conducted for legitimate purposes and in an apparently legitimate manner, will fall foul of legal rules. One such rule is the *ultra vires* doctrine, which I will consider a little later. But there are other areas in which there is legal uncertainty which is damaging to the markets. One of them is the characterisation of transactions and the risk of recharacterisation according to their perceived economic substance rather than their legal content. That is a matter I shall be discussing next week. Another is the concern that netting under rules of clearing systems will fall foul of insolvency law, leaving a liquidator free to cherry-pick, adopting a transaction that is profitable while disclaiming the unprofitable countervailing transaction. That concern has been addressed by special provisions in the Companies Act 1989 by which the netting procedures of an exchange or clearing house related to market, money market and related contracts are rendered immune from attack under insolvency law and are given precedence over insolvency procedures relating to proof and set-off.[43] This issue is considered of such importance that there is to be a European Union Settlement Finality Directive requiring Member States (*inter alia*) to ensure that insolvency does not render netting unenforceable or liable to unwinding.[44] A further interesting development is the central importance now attached to legal opinions on the validity of transactions. The furnishing of such opinions has long been a condition of cross-border loans and bond issues and in relation to netting it is now required by the European Solvency Ratio Directive[45] and the Bank of England as a condition of recognising netting as risk reduction for capital adequacy purposes.

The *ultra vires* rule and the problem of market confidence

I shall conclude this lecture by looking at the tension between market interest and public interest in the context of the powers of local authorities to engage in commercial transactions; and I shall take as my illustration the much-discussed decision of the House of Lords in *Hazell v. Hammersmith and Fulham London Borough Council*.[46] The story is well known.[47] In company with many other local authorities the Hammersmith and Fulham

---

[43] Companies Act 1989, s.159.
[44] Draft Directive 9962/97 on settlement finality in payment and securities settlement systems, September 26, 1997.
[45] Directive 89/647 dated December 18, 1989, as amended.
[46] [1992] 2 A.C. 1.
[47] For an instructive account, see Ewan McKendrick, "Local Authorities and Swaps: Undermining the Market?" in *Making Commercial Law* (ed. Ross Cranston), Chap. 9.

London Borough Council decided to enter the swaps market. What distinguished this particular authority's swaps operations was their sheer number and magnitude, which exceeded those of all the other authorities put together. The total commitments were many times the local authority's annual budget on its other functions. Concern was expressed by the Audit Commission about the legality of these transactions. Junior counsel advised that entry into swaps was beyond the powers of local authorities; leading counsel, that swaps that were entered into as part of interest-risk management and limited to the total of an authority's indebtedness or underlying transactions were lawful. In view of the legal uncertainties an interim strategy was adopted to engage in further transactions to reduce expose to interest-rate rises pending clarification of the legal position. Ultimately all swap operations were terminated.

The auditor sought a declaration from the Divisional Court that all the transactions were *ultra vires*. It was accepted that local authorities had no power to borrow except as provided by the Local Government Act 1972 and that the Act conferred no express power to engage in swap transactions. But Schedule 13 to the Act authorised local authorities to borrow and to re-finance borrowings, and the banks contended that swaps were covered by section 111(1) of the Act as "calculated to facilitate" or "conducive or incidental to" the discharge of the borrowing function. The Divisional Court made the declaration sought by the auditor, a declaration binding on those banks who had intervened in the proceedings, with the result that payments due to them under the offending swap agreements would be irrecoverable. The Court of Appeal took the view that the transactions were lawful so far as (a) they were engaged in for the purpose of debt management and took the form of "parallel contracts" (that is, they were linked to identifiable borrowings), or (b) they were designed to mitigate, through the interim strategy, the adverse effects of unlawful transactions entered into in good faith, but that all other transactions were speculative trading transactions and were *ultra vires*. The House of Lords restored the decision of the Divisional Court, holding that swap transactions were neither calculated to facilitate nor conducive or incidental to the local authority's borrowing function, and all of them were *ultra vires*.

It is clear from the speeches of Lord Templeman and Lord Ackner that this decision was powerfully motivated by their view that all swaps, even those designed to reduce exposure under existing borrowing obligations, were speculative in character. The argument advanced by the banks that swaps were akin to insurance against risk was robustly rejected by Lord Templeman:

> "A swap contract based on a notional principal sum of £1m under which the local authority promises to pay the bank £10,000 if LIBOR rises by one per cent and the bank promises to pay the local authority £10,000 if LIBOR falls by one per cent is more akin to gambling than insurance."[48]

Similarly, the argument that swaps could be regarded as replacement contracts and were therefore a form of debt management received short shrift from Lord Ackner. The original underlying debts, he said, continued in existence and were therefore unaffected by the swaps transactions. Moreover, if interest rates moved adversely to the local authority's swap position it would have wasted transaction costs and, in addition, it bore the credit risk of default by its counter-party.[49] So the entire series of swap agreements was struck down—a striking contrast with the approach of Lord Denning in the *Kirkwood*[50] case.

The difference of view between the House of Lords and the Court of Appeal provides a vivid illustration of the continuing battle between form and substance.[51] The House of Lords took the position that hedging by means of a swap is not debt management, for the original debt still remains; a swap therefore produces an effect essentially different from a refinancing. That, of course, is quite true from a technical legal viewpoint, but it does not reflect the commercial reality where the counter-party to the hedge is of undoubted financial stability. The Court of Appeal, by contrast, looked to the commercial effect in the particular case of the underlying transaction and the linked swap in combination. In the words of Sir Stephen Brown P.:

> "Of course, entering into a swap transaction with reference to a particular debt does not have the effect of law of altering the rate of

[48] [1992] 2 A.C. 1 at 34–35.
[49] *ibid.*, at 45–46.
[50] [1960] 2 Q.B. 431. See *ante*, p. 40.
[51] See generally Paul Goris, *The Legal Aspect of Swaps* (1994), which devotes considerable attention to the form versus substance issue in relation to swaps dealings.

interest payable by the local authority as borrower to the lender. But commercially, the combined effect of the original loan and the swap transaction is the same as if the interest rate in the actual loan has been varied. In theory there is a risk that the party to the swap transaction might become insolvent or default for some other reason but with the parties of the standing of the banks and other parties involved in the swap transactions under challenge, that credit risk is more theoretical than real."[52]

Now one can understand well enough the concern of the House of Lords to secure the protection of ratepayers against misuse of public funds. But there is force in the criticism that to isolate a hedging transaction from the underlying borrowing to which it is linked, and thereby to conclude that it is simply another form of speculation akin to gambling, is to fly in the face of reality and of market usage. As the Court of Appeal correctly pointed out, every commercial transaction has a pricing risk. If the test of speculation is the risk of an adverse movement in interest rates, without regard to any hedging operation, then all lending and borrowing, whether at a fixed rate or a floating rate, constitutes speculation. Indeed, the same is true of every purchase and sale, of every lease and hire agreement, indeed of every commercial transaction one can possibly think of. On this test an insured risk is as speculative as an uninsured risk. There is a delicious irony in the fact that only last month two leading economists, Professors Robert Merton and Myron Scholes, were awarded the Nobel prize for devising pricing models for derivatives trading which, in the words of *The Economist*, "turned risk management from a guessing game into a science".

The decision in *Hammersmith and Fulham* caused such damage to London's reputation as a world financial centre that the Bank of England set up the Legal Risk Review Committee to consider steps that might be taken to alleviate anxieties resulting from uncertainty as to the legality of transactions. One of these was the establishment of the Financial Law Panel, which periodically issues reports offering advice on issues affecting the markets on which there is legal uncertainty. It is clear that at least some members of the House of Lords as currently constituted are aware of the serious harm inflicted by the ruling in the *Hammersmith and Fulham* case, of which Lord Goff, in the subsequent decision in *Westdeutsche*, observed:

[52] [1990] 2 Q.B. 697 at 780.

"It is unnecessary for present purposes to examine the basis of that decision, though I wish to record that it caused grave concern among financial institutions, and especially foreign banks, which had entered into such transactions with local authorities in good faith, with no idea that a rule as technical as the *ultra vires* doctrine might undermine what they saw as a perfectly legitimate commercial transaction."[53]

If the decision in *Hammersmith and Fulham* had such an impact in an environment where there was no organised market in swaps, deals being concluded by bilateral agreement with or through a bank, it does not take much imagination to appreciate the potential for an even graver, domino effect if there had been an organised swaps market with multilateral clearing and settlement and the consequent need to unwind failed transactions across the entire day's dealings. One might add that ordinary imprudent borrowing can have just as devastating an effect on a local authority's finances, yet the Local Government Act provides that:

"A person lending money to a local authority shall not be bound to enquire whether the borrowing of the money is legal or regular or whether the money raised was properly applied and shall not be prejudiced by any illegality or irregularity, or by the misapplication or non-application of any of that money."[54]

The way forward is surely to make this provision one of general application, separating the internal powers of local authorities from their external relationships and abolishing the *ultra vires* doctrine altogether.[55] In this way the law can be brought into harmony with the legitimate needs of commerce, and faith restored in the legal stability of operations on London's financial markets.

[53] [1996] A.C. 669 at 680.
[54] Sched. 14, para. 20.
[55] As has virtually been done in relation to registered companies by s.35 of the Companies Act 1985, pursuant to E.C. legislation.

3. Property Rights in Commercial Assets: Rethinking Concepts and Policies

I INTRODUCTION

All legal systems have a concept of property. The concept varies
from one legal system to another, and even within a single legal
system it is peculiarly difficult to define or even to describe.
Nevertheless the distinction between property and obligation,
between what I own and what I am owed, is a fundamental
principle of our jurisprudence and is of central importance in
commercial law. English law adopts a liberal attitude towards
the acquisition and transfer of proprietary rights in personal
property, to the point that by a single agreement perfected by a
single registration a company can give a global covering all its
assets present and future. For some reason the criminal law
applies different concepts. So in the curious case of *R. v. Preddy*[1]
the House of Lords held that a person who by false statements
procured loans from a building society could not be convicted of
obtaining property by deception since the inter-bank payment
mechanism did not involve the transfer of any chose in action,
merely a debit to the building society's account which was
reflected in a credit to the defendant's account. This decision
came as a surprise to most of us, since in the civil law the
proprietary remedy resulting from tracing in equity does not
depend on the transfer of an asset from plaintiff to defendant,
only from its improper receipt at the plaintiff's expense. Apart
from this criminal law quirk, which necessitated emergency
legislation,[2] proprietary rights in English law are exceptionally
well developed.

Yet interests in personal property remain an area of acute
difficulty in English law, largely because of the inadequacy of

[1] [1996] 1 A.C. 815.
[2] Theft (Amendment) Act 1996.

our conceptual treatment of the subject[3] and because, in contrast with other jurisdictions, we have made no attempt to introduce up-to-date, comprehensive legislation to reflect modern commercial needs and practices. A great deal has changed even over the past two decades. In relation to contracts for the sale of goods the law has had to grapple with claims to an interest in commingled products and with floating bailments in which the bailee is given a right to substitute new equipment for old. In the field of investment securities we have moved steadily from paper-based to book-entry systems of issue and transfer, from direct holdings to indirect holdings through a nominee, fund manager or custodian, and from indirect holdings in an identified security to co-ownership holdings in securities pools. Moreover, the collateralisation of overnight and other very short-term finance provided by the sale and repurchase of securities ("repo") and of redelivery obligations arising from stock lending necessitates a speedy and sophisticated mechanism for the creation and perfection of transitory security interests.

The principal focus of my talk this evening is on the characterisation of transactions relating to personal property. I shall begin by assuming that a person has transferred a property interest and discuss how the law characterises the transaction and how in policy terms it ought to be characterised. For example, is a transaction in the form of a stock loan or a sale and repurchase of investments (a "repo") to be characterised according to its form or should the law look to the economic substance and regard it as a form of secured lending? Should a finance lease be treated in law as a lease or as a sale and, if the latter, should the lessor's retention of title be equated with a security interest? I shall then move on to a still more fundamental question: whether transactions of different types do in fact confer a property interest at all. This will be examined in the context, first, of charge-backs, that is, instruments expressed to confer on a bank a charge over its own customer' credit balance and, secondly, of claims to co-ownership and co-security rights in a bulk of goods and in a pool of investment securities.

I do not propose to engage in a detailed technical exposition of a very complex area of law, though some reference to

---

[3] Scottish lawyers, influenced by the Roman law tradition, have always been more engaged of concepts in personal property than their English counterparts. See, for example, Professor Kenneth Reid's excellent *Law of Property in Scotland* (1996).

concepts and conceptual problems can scarcely be avoided; my concern is rather with the policy implications of the present law. Should we continue to categorise property rights according to their form rather than their substance or move to a functional approach based on the economic purpose and effect of a transaction? If the latter, is this a task that can safely be left to the courts or is it better left to statute? And if we are to have legislation, do we need categorisation at all? Would it not be sufficient for the statute to lay down rules governing what is to happen in typical cases? The treatment of claims to a share of pooled investment securities is a matter of great importance raising special concerns. The question to be answered here is whether we can continue to muddle along with a combination of contract, equity and trusts or whether we should not go back to the drawing board and enact legislation specifically designed for dealings in investment securities.

Finally, I shall consider very briefly whether the concept of property in English law has not become over-expansive, to the detriment or potential detriment of the general body of creditors of an insolvent enterprise.

The significance of characterisation and property concepts

Before we embark on the first two of these groups of issues it is worth asking why they matter. Of course, for an academic it is not necessary that they *should* matter! Still, it is comforting to think that now and then one is able to discuss something of more than purely theoretical interest, particularly to a gathering that includes so many practitioners. In the commercial law course at Oxford we spend a good deal of time on characterisation questions; and we do so not merely for their intrinsic intellectual interest but because they are of immense practical importance and raise what is a recurrent theme of these lectures, the battle between form and substance. Upon the characterisation of a transaction may turn, among other things, the registrability of an interest as a security interest, the treatment of the transaction in the respective balance sheets of the contracting parties, the taxation implications, the question whether the transaction does or does not breach a negative pledge clause in a loan agreement, its efficacy in the event of the insolvency of one of the parties, and the impact of the transaction on the calculation of assets and liabilities for the purpose of determining compliance with capital adequacy requirements. Similarly, the distinction between property rights and personal rights is of vital importance if the obligor becomes insolvent, for the holder of a property right can enforce it ahead of the general body of creditors, whereas the holder of a personal right can only prove for a dividend in competition with other creditors. And the wheels of fortune can change so rapidly that scarcely any institution, however respectable or prestigious, is immune from the risk of insolvency, whether through market forces, incompetence or otherwise. We have only to look at what happened to the great banking house of Baring to appreciate this.

II   THE CHARACTERISATION OF PROPERTY TRANSACTIONS

In the world of commerce the form versus substance argument has traditionally surfaced in the characterisation of transactions creating property rights. I will discuss two only: whether in policy terms transactions in the form of a conditional sale agreement, finance lease, sale and repurchase or stock loan should be treated as what they purport to be or should be dealt with as a security agreement; and whether we should continue to retain the floating charge as a category of security. I shall say something about each of these in turn.

Sale, lease or security?

In law a conditional sale agreement is simply an agreement for sale in which the seller reserves title until payment. The buyer is not considered to give security, because the asset does not belong to him until he has paid for it. The same applies to hire-purchase agreements, where the hirer has the option, but not the obligation, to buy. Similarly, in dealing with the sale and repurchase of assets, the courts have disregarded the economic substance of the transaction and have taken the line that so long as it is genuine and not a disguised chattel mortgage it will be given effect according to its terms. Rather surprisingly there has been no case law on the repo or the stock loan, to which, however, similar principles must apply. In the repo, securities are sold upon terms that the seller will repurchase the securities or others of the same kind the following day or within a short period. A primary purpose of the transaction is to enable securities dealers to obtain overnight or other short-term

financing to repay intra-day advances from their banks. In the
stock loan, the owner of securities lends them to another person
who is short of the stock on terms that the latter will redeliver
the equivalent securities at a later date, the redelivery obligation
being collateralised by the transfer to the lender of cash, bonds
or different stock, with power to the borrower to substitute
alternative collateral of equal value, and the lender must then
redeliver the equivalent when the original stock loan is discharged. The stock loan can be distinguished from the repo by
its underlying purpose and by the fact that there is no money
price involved, but both involve a transfer from A to B and a
transfer back from B to A and, where the collateral is cash, the
net effect of the stock loan is almost indistinguishable from that
of a repo.

Let us now cross the Atlantic and see how matters developed
there. The time-price doctrine was picked up and fairly consistently applied in American decisions. Eventually the Uniform
Commercial Code came into being and the draftsmen, having
originally planned to treat separately conditional sale, leases
with option to purchase, trust receipts and chattel mortgages, hit
on the brilliant and conceptually simple device of treating all of
them as secured transactions, on the basis that in each case the
agreement was intended to fulfil a security function, so that, for
example, the seller's reservation of title was to be limited to a
security interest, the buyer was to be treated as if he were the
owner giving security and the security interest was to be
registrable in the same way as if it had been a chattel mortgage.
Thus did the genius of American law-making light upon a
functional, integrated approach to security which cut through
the doctrinal tangles and largely obliterated the traditional
distinction between the grant of security and title reservation.

As I have said earlier, the accountancy profession takes a
different view on all these matters—one more closely allied to
the functional approach of American law—to which I shall
shortly refer. To the accountant the economic value of the asset
belongs to the buyer or lessee, and in substance both the
conditional sale agreement and the finance lease are to be
equated with an outright sale in which the asset is shown as that
of the buyer or lessee and the liability for future instalments or
rentals is to be capitalised in the buyer's or lessee's balance
sheet. Similarly, sale and repurchase are treated as secured loans
in which the asset remains on the seller's balance sheet. The

accountancy treatment thus matches fairly closely the legal treatment under Article 9 of the American Uniform Commercial Code, except, however, that it fails to show the link between the liability and the asset, and thus the secured status of the seller— a matter of complete indifference so long as the company remains solvent but highly significant if it goes into liquidation.

Recharacterisation

Should we now follow the North American model and recharacterise these transactions according to their economic substance rather than their legal form? And if so, is this a task for the courts or for Parliament? Let me begin with conditional sale, hire-purchase and finance lease agreements. There can be no doubt at all that the reform of English personal property security law is long overdue. We have one legal regime for hire-purchase, a different one for conditional sale, a third for mortgages, a fourth for equitable charges and a fifth for pledges. The retention of title under hire-purchase and conditional sale agreements is intended as security but is not so treated in law, with the result that it is not registrable and is therefore invisible to other financiers. The existence of five different legal regimes causes endless complications and involves industry, commerce and banking in needless cost and delay. Article 9 of the Uniform Commercial Code replaces all these and other security devices with a single security interest perfected by a single filing or by possession. The Canadians, having introduced similar legislation some 20 years ago, are now as enthusiastic as the Americans. The registration systems now in use in Canada are efficient, cheap and self-financing—indeed, they earn a healthy profit. The case for an enactment along the lines of Article 9 is overwhelming. As far back as 1971 the Crowther Committee on Consumer Credit recommended the adoption of a simplified version of Article 9, a recommendation later endorsed by the Cork Report on Insolvency and the Diamond Report on Security Interests in Property. Unhappily, legislation has yet to be introduced.

It would be possible for the move towards a functional approach to be taken by the courts. In the United States the courts are much readier than our own to ignore the legal form of a transaction and characterise it according to its economic effect. But I believe that our courts, located as they are in the world's leading financial centre, have shown great wisdom in adhering to the formal approach to characterisation of trans-actions where these are genuine and are designed to fulfil a legitimate business objective.

In the first place, courts are not well equipped to evolve their own criteria for evaluating economic substance, and their eval-uations will inevitably be so fact-oriented, so dependent on a case-by-case assessment of the relevant factors, as to generate a high degree of uncertainty. In addition, the powers of courts are circumscribed; it is not as open to them as it is to the legislature to declare, for example, that all leases for a period exceeding a year will be deemed to constitute security agreements or that a recharacterisation will be for a limited purpose, for example by treating sales of accounts as security agreements solely for the purpose of registration. On characterisation issues bright lines are best laid down by the legislature; and if the legislature fails to do this adequately then parties are again thrown back on the courts' own evaluations. Particular care is needed to ensure clarity in the treatment of leases.

These points are highlighted by the recent decision in *American President Lines Ltd v. Lykes Steamship Co. Inc.*[4] In that case the United States Bankruptcy District for the Middle District of Florida characterised as a secured transaction what appeared on traditional criteria to be a true lease of some ships, with severe consequences for the "lessor" in a transaction involving hun-dreds of millions of dollars. This has prompted strong criticism of the test of "economic reality", on the ground that this phrase conveys an impression of an authoritative, logical and sensible process of characterisation, whereas in truth it involves a series of subjective inferences, understandings and meanings of com-plex contractual language and simply substitutes one mental construct for another.[5] The decision graphically illustrates the problems that arise where courts have to balance conflicting economic considerations rather than apply formal legal criteria. These problems are exacerbated where the test laid down by the legislature and applied by the courts differs from the tax or accounting treatment. In recognition of these problems Article 9 was amended to provide a brighter line for the courts and this has gone a long way to resolving the problem.

---

[4] (1996) 196 Bank.R. 574.
[5] Austin, Schwartz and Lenkowsky, "A Question of Character", *Asset Finance and Leasing Digest* (July/August 1996), p. 23; and "Revision Urgently Required", *ibid.* (September 1996), p. 22.

Secondly, case law in this country operates retrospectively; we do not possess that useful instrument of change fashioned by the United States Supreme Court, the doctrine of prospective overruling, by which the decision affects only the case in issue and future transactions but does not disturb what has gone before. So any major change in the judicial approach to characterisation could have serious consequences for parties to thousands of transactions. A case in point is the decision handed down in 1963 by the Supreme Court of Nebraska in *Elder v. Doerr*,[6] where the court, disregarding a long line of previous authority, held that the finance charge was in the nature of interest and the rate was usurious. In vain did the plaintiff plead that the rate was within the ceiling set by the Nebraska Retail Installment Sales Act 1959. Though this was true the court held the Act void on the ground that it contravened a provision of the Nebraska constitution prohibiting special legislation regulating interest. The decision was said to have rendered irrecoverable all sums due under retail instalment sales contracts since the passing of the Act, estimated to amount in total to what was then the huge sum of $400 million dollars. The result was that instalment credit trading in Nebraska ground to a halt. There then followed a series of enactments, each designed to put the matter right and each in turn being struck down as invalid. Only on the eighth attempt by the legislature did the Supreme Court finally profess itself satisfied.[7] A cautionary tale indeed!

We can conclude, therefore, that while, in the field of security in personal property, transactions should be regulated according to their economic function and effect and not according to their legal form, this is the province of the legislature, not of the courts. Let us hope that after all these years parliamentary time will be found to give effect to this part of the 26-year-old Crowther Report.

What of the repo and the stock loan? In my view these are not as such security agreements even in economic terms, for in both cases ownership passes on the initial transfer and if there were nothing more the transferor would have no proprietary interest

---

[6] 175 Nebraska 483, 122 NW 2d 528 (1963). See R.M. Goode and Jacob S. Ziegel, *Hire-Purchase and Conditional Sale: A Comparative Survey of Commonwealth and American Law* (1965).

[7] For details, see Barbara Curran, *Trends in Consumer Credit Legislation* (1965), pp. 88–89.

until completion of the reverse transaction. What does give rise to the grant of security is the practice of requiring the transferee to furnish collateral for its reverse obligation. It is possible, though in my view unlikely, that the borrower's power to substitute equivalent collateral converts the security into a floating charge so as to be registrable under the Companies Act. It would be as well to make it clear in legislation that a mere power of substitution does not have this effect. To require extremely short-term securities to be placed on the register and then almost immediately afterwards removed would be absurd. The desirability of legislation is brought out by the treatment of repos and stock lending in American law. Curiously, despite the length and detail of its definition of "security interest", Article 9 of the Uniform Commercial Code makes no attempt to offer a characterisation of the repo or the stock loan, and the Prefatory Note to the revised Article 8, which deals with investment securities, disclaims any attempt to deal with the matter. The burden has thus fallen on the courts to do what they can without any specific guidance. The case law is divided, some courts upholding the form of the transaction, others ruling on the basis of what they perceive as the economic substance. We would do well to take measures to avoid any risk of the latter.

Fixed or floating charge?

This bring me to the distinction between a fixed charge, in which the creditor contractually controls the disposal of the charged assets, and the floating charge, where the debtor company is left free to dispose of the charged assets in the ordinary course of business free from the security interest. The distinction is relevant to priorities between the charge holder and subsequent incumbrancers and is also material to the priority of the charge over preferential creditors in a winding-up or receivership.

After the decision of Hoffmann J. in *Re Brightlife Ltd*[8] I thought I had finally conquered the mysteries of the floating charge. Vain hope! There came a series of case, culminating in *Re New Bullas Ltd*,[9] which I have to confess have left me as confused as my students. What *Re New Bullas Ltd* decided was that the

[8] [1987] Ch. 200.
[9] [1994] 1 B.C.L.C. 485.

parties were free, if they so wished, to agree that a fixed charge be given over book debts while leaving the proceeds of collection at the disposal of the chargor. I have discussed the case elsewhere[10] and need not spend time on it now. It is a further example of the triumph of form over function. What we have not yet come to realise in this country is that the floating charge, brilliant though it was in conception, has now outlived its usefulness. Recently a group of judges and academics from Bulgaria visited Oxford. They were fascinated by the intellectual subtleties of the floating charge, which they were anxious to understand. In my very first consciously unpatriotic act I urged them not to emulate our example, which would involve an assessment and understanding of countless cases and innumerable commentaries. I pointed out that Article 9 of the Uniform Commercial Code resolves the competing interests in a simple and elegant fashion, by providing, in effect, that the debtor's power of disposal is not inconsistent with a fixed security interest but that the buyer of inventory takes free from the security interest, even if knowing of it, unless he also knows that the disposition to him is in breach of the security agreement.[11] That is the path that we ourselves should follow.

III PROPERTY AND OBLIGATION

So far we have assumed that a person has a property right and that the question is how, as a matter of policy, the law should characterise it. But the distinction between what I own and what I am owed is far from clear cut. I want to look first at charge-backs and secondly at claims to co-ownership or co-security interests in a bulk of goods or a pool of investment securities.

Charge-backs

Can a bank take an effective charge over its own customer's credit balance or does this amount to a contractual set-off and not a true security at all? This question, which in most cases is of no practical importance whatsoever, and is therefore of the utmost interest to academics, has generated a huge controversy.

---

[10] "Charges over Book Debts—A Missed Opportunity" (1994) 110 L.Q.R. 592.
[11] See Goode, "The Exodus of the Floating Charge" in *Corporate and Commercial Law* (eds Feldman and Meisel, 1996), Chap. 10.

I have to plead guilty to the serious charge that I was myself
responsible for starting this hare when, in a little book published
in 1982, I suggested that a bank as debtor could not become its
own creditor and that for it to be given a charge over its own
obligation was conceptually impossible. This approach was
adopted four years later by Millett J. in *Re Charge Card Services
Ltd*,[12] a decision subsequently endorsed by the Court of Appeal
(albeit by way of *obiter dicta*) in *Re Bank of Credit and Commerce
International SA (No. 8)*,[13] but disapproved by the House of
Lords.[14] Lord Hoffmann, giving the substantive speech, concluded that there was no reason why a bank could not take a
charge over its customer's deposit. Again, this was strictly an
obiter dictum, though obviously it is of the highest persuasive
value.

Lord Hoffmann's speech is interesting in showing how a
determined jurist can surmount apparently insuperable conceptual problems in order to arrive at what he perceives to be a
sensible commercial result. To reach his conclusion Lord
Hoffmann had to give a new meaning to the concept of a
proprietary interest,[15] to recognise as a charge a contractual
entitlement which could be exercised only by book-entry, not by
any of the established methods of realisation, and to postulate a
chargee who had no one to sue (the chargee being itself the
debtor) and no asset capable of being sold or followed into the
hands of a third party. Finally, it was necessary to deal with the
awkward decision of the House of Lords in *National Westminster
Bank Ltd v. Halesowen Presswork and Assemblies Ltd*,[16] in which
Viscount Dilhorne and Lord Cross specifically approved the
statement of Buckley L.J. in the Court of Appeal that no man
could have a lien on his own property and that it could not be
said with any kind of accuracy that the bank had a lien on its
own indebtedness to its customer.[17] These speeches, which on
any ordinary reading must surely have meant exactly what they
said, were swept aside as directed to a different issue, namely
the inability to exercise a lien over intangible property.

---

[12] [1987] Ch. 150.
[13] [1996] Ch. 245.
[14] [1997] 4 All E.R. 568.
[15] "It [the asserted charge] would be a proprietary interest in the sense that . . . it
would be binding upon assignees or a liquidator or trustee in bankruptcy"
ibid., at 577.
[16] [1972] A.C. 785.
[17] [1971] 1 Q.B. 1 at 46.

It will be apparent that I have considerable difficulty with the conceptual reasoning which led Lord Hoffmann to conclude that he was doing nothing out of the way in upholding a bank's ability to take a charge over its own indebtedness to its customer.[18] The problem is compounded by the fact that the policy issues were simply not explored at all; indeed, it was said that there were none. In fact there was a serious policy question to be considered, that is, whether contracting parties, by the mere device of attaching the label "charge" to a document which provided a means of "realisation" indistinguishable from that used to effect a contractual set-off, should be able to bypass all the restrictions on insolvent set-off (including the admissibility of set-off of claims against third parties) to the detriment of the general body of creditors. It is ironic that a decision intended to be a policy-based response to perceived commercial needs should furnish yet another example of the triumph of form over substance in English law.

Now the traditional way of overcoming obstructive concepts is by the use of a legal fiction. Both Church and State, which at one time equated all interest with usury, were forced by economic pressures to modify the rigour of this approach, which they did by the simple device of excluding from account that part of the interest which reflected the risk to the lender, so that over time usury came to mean excessive interest. We continue to use a number of fictions in our law—for example, terms implied by law and the notional continuance of security in favour of a surety who has repaid the debt. Civil law systems, to preserve the concept that pledge depends on possession, treat registration or book-entry of interests in intangibles as constituting possession.[19] The difficulty for a court is in openly acknowledging that it is creating a fiction; hence the advantage of legislation, which can openly declare that X is deemed to be Y without our having to say that X *is* Y. But as Professor Lon

---

[18] I have deployed my arguments more extensively in a case note in (1998) 114 L.Q.R. 8.

[19] Even the European Union has its legal fictions. A regulation was drafted providing that a product was not to be labelled jam unless it contained fruit. Consternation in Portugal over the very popular jam made with carrots. This was surmounted by the simple device of redesignating carrot as a fruit! See Directive 88/593 (dated November 18, 1988), art. 1(13), amending Directive 79/693 (dated July 24, 1979), Annex II(A)(1). This solution works well enough so long as we are not beguiled into thinking that carrot *is* a fruit.

Fuller wrote in his classic work on legal fictions, a proposed
legal fiction should receive consideration as but one step in the
reasoning process and should be subjected to possible correc-
tives,[20] such as, in this case, the fundamentality of the concept
that is being set aside, the magnitude of the problem which the
fiction seeks to overcome (which was acknowledged to be slight,
since there were other ways of attaining the desired result) and
the policy objection to which I have referred. Moreover, the
solution offered raises problems of its own to which I have
alluded elsewhere.[21]   So we need to exercise a degree of caution
before eroding so fundamental a concept as the distinction
between property and obligation.

Co-ownership and co-security rights

I now turn to consider rights of ownership or security held or
supposedly held by a person in common with others. There are
two distinct inquiries. The first is the manner in which a person
who did not previously hold any interest in the components of
an asset or asset pool can acquire such an interest. The second is
what happens when a person who does hold an interest in an
asset transfers it into a common pool. Does he thereby give up
all property rights or does he acquire an interest in common in
the pool? These questions are not purely technical; they raise
policy considerations which in my view have yet to be adequately addressed.

Interests in common in new assets

If a transaction is to be relied on as giving a person an interest in
common with others in an asset or asset pool to which he has
not himself contributed, two conditions have normally to be
satisfied: he must have bargained for such an interest, and he
must be able to identify the subject-matter of the bargain. Thus
section 16 of the Sale of Goods Act 1979 states that under a
contract for the sale of unascertained goods the property does
not pass until they have been ascertained. That is not simply a
rule of law, it is an inescapable fact of life: I must be able to
identify what I claim to own. Not only is a proprietary claim to
wholly unascertained goods doomed to failure, as was agreed

[20] See also *ante*, p. 27.
[21] (1998) 114 L.Q.R. 8 at 11.

by all the judges in the *Goldcorp* case,[22] but it is not even sufficient that the contractual source of supply is identified; it is necessary that the agreed quantity to be taken from that supply shall have been unconditionally appropriated to my contract, usually by an act such as dispatch via an independent carrier which places the goods outside the seller's control. The effect of the Act in its original form was that if I paid in advance for 99 bottles of wine to be supplied from a stock of 100 bottles and my seller became bankrupt I could not claim ownership of a single bottle, for it could not be predicated of any individual bottle that it was not the one bottle excluded from my purchase. Because of that one bottle outstanding I was merely an unsecured creditor. But if, before the seller's bankruptcy, one bottle had rolled off the shelf and smashed, I would then have become the owner of the remaining 99 bottles. And I could have avoided the whole problem if, instead of contracting to buy 99 bottles, I had agreed to purchase a 99 per cent interest in the entire collection of 100 bottles.

This distinction between agreeing to buy an unidentified part of a whole and agreeing to buy an interest in the entire bulk was thought to be so technical, and the outcome so contrary to legitimate expectation, that the Act was changed to provide in section 20A that the prepaying buyer of a part interest in a bulk will be at any given time co-owner of the bulk in the proportion that the quantity of goods remaining to be delivered to him bears to the bulk still remaining at that time. For some reason section 16 was amended to make it subject to section 20A, as if the latter created an exception to the requirement of ascertainment, which of course it does not and cannot. What section 20A does is to make the subject-matter of the contract the bulk itself, instead of the unidentified quantity to be taken from it, so that the requirement of ascertainment is satisfied. The losers from this change are, of course, the seller's unsecured creditors. But supporters of the change would argue that they have not really lost anything, for section 20A applies only to the extent that the goods have been prepaid: they have merely been deprived of what was previously an unjust enrichment, a double benefit by which the seller's estate both received the price of the goods and retained the goods themselves.

However, this statutory regime is confined to contracts for the sale of goods; it does not apply to other types of dealing, such as

[22] *Re Goldcorp Exchange Ltd* [1995] 1 A.C. 74.

a mortgage, nor does it apply to the sale or other disposition of intangibles, such as securities or debts. For this reason the decision of the Court of Appeal in *Hunter v. Moss*,[23] upholding the ruling of the trial judge that a declaration of trust as to 50 out of 1000 registered shares in a company created a valid trust, has been criticised. The case was no different, say the critics, from a trust or agreement relating to 50 out of 100 bottles of wine or 50 out of 100 tons of potatoes, which cannot take effect until there has been segregation of the contract quantity from the bulk. In my view the decision was correct. Shares, being intangible, are not like wine or potatoes, for these can be segregated and removed from the bulk, whereas shares, though transferable, are incapable of segregation from the rest of the share capital. English law, technical though it may be, does not demand a condition of ownership which it is impossible to fulfil.[24] So a trust of 50 out of 1000 issued shares is no more than a trust of 5 per cent of the share capital. Section 20A is confined to contracts of sale of goods and does not extend to documentary intangibles, such as bearer securities or negotiable instruments; but since these are by their nature perfected, and expected to be perfected, by delivery, there is no great call for such an extension.

Interests in pooled assets generally

Let us now look at the position where a person owning an item of personal property, such as goods or shares, transfers ownership to another in the knowledge that what was previously his asset is to be commingled with assets belonging to the transferee or to third parties. For example, a number of people owning gold deliver their gold holdings to a refiner to be made up into bullion and returned to them in the form of gold bars. If the refinery goes into liquidation before the depositors of the gold have received their entitlements, are they owners in common of the gold held by the refinery or merely unsecured creditors? The answer, as correctly given by the New Zealand Court of Appeal in *Coleman v. Harvey*,[25] is that it depends on the parties' express

[23] [1994] 3 All E.R. 215.
[24] Regulation 25 of the Uncertificated Securities Regulations 1995 (S.I. 1995 No. 3272), though infelicitous in its wording, must, it is thought, have the same effect.
[25] [1989] 1 N.Z.L.R. 723.

or presumed intention. If the gold bars are required to be supplied from the bulk contributed by the different depositors, then the inference is that until delivery to them of the contract quantities due to them they are to be co-owners of the bulk in the proportions of their respective interests. The example here given relates to gold but would be equally true of any other kind of deposited asset, such as coins and notes, securities or oil and gas.

In each case the relevant fact is the character of the depositee; and we begin to get some idea of the sophistication of owner-ship concepts in modern commercial law when we see that even a depositee to whom legal title has been transferred can occupy any one of no fewer than four different capacities, each with different legal effects. He can be a custodian of a fungible pool of assets or of an escrow account who, though the legal owner of the individual assets comprising the pool or the sums deposited in the account, is a bare trustee with neither the right to apply them for his own purposes nor powers of management on behalf of the depositors; he can be a trustee or fund manager of a fund consisting of the assets from time to time held on deposit, in which case he has dealing powers which, however, are not those of an absolute owner but are circumscribed by the terms of the fund management agreement or trust deed, so that he cannot apply the deposited assets for his own purposes; he can be a mortgagee under a transfer of ownership by way of security, with a duty to retransfer when the mortgage is redeemed; or he can be a banker, whether of money, securities, oil and gas or any other kind of asset, obtaining full ownership and thus having the freedom to treat the asset as his own, with a mere personal obligation to restore its equivalent. Deposit of assets with a person as banker involves a legal risk that does not arise in the other three categories of deposit, namely that if he becomes insolvent the deposited assets form part of his estate so as to be distributable among his general creditors so far as not picked up in another creditor's security. This is as true of the banking of oil and gas as it is of the banking of money. That is why the question of characterisation of the depositor's rights is of such immense practical importance in domestic and inter-national finance. And nowhere is it of greater importance than in relation to pools of investment securities.

Interests in dematerialised or immobilised securities

The pooling of securities, in which a custodian's nominee company holds in its own name, but segregated from its own funds, securities belonging to different clients without separate designation of their individual interests, has long been a feature of fund management. It possesses several advantages over individual client designation, including simplification of accounts, economies of scale in transposing investments and acceleration of the settlement process. And this brings me to the revolution that has been taking place in the arrangements for issue, transfer and custody of securities. To reduce the volume of paper involved in the issue of certificates and the completion and lodgment of transfer forms, two distinct mechanisms have evolved, dematerialisation and immobilisation.

Let me begin with dematerialisation. Systems have been devised under statutory authority for uncertificated securities to be issued, whether by way of a new issue to system-members or to any holder in replacement of certificated securities, and for transfers to be effected by electronic means through the relevant system. The Central Gilts Office has for some time had a system in place for uncertificated dealings in gilt-edged securities, and this is now available for equities and bonds through CREST. However, this dematerialisation of registered securities does not change the rules of law governing the transfer of legal title, which continues to be effected by an entry on the issuer's register, though the register must identify separately certificated and uncertificated holdings. There is, however, a special rule in the regulations that equitable title to uncertificated units vests in the intended transferee when an operator-instruction is generated requiring the participating issuer to register the transfer.[26] Bearer securities continue to be transferable by delivery in the usual way unless and until surrendered for conversion into registered securities. Beyond this, dematerialisation appears to have little or no impact on property rights in securities except, of course, that dematerialised securities share with paper-based registered securities the characteristic that they are not negotiable.

Of much greater significance for our purposes is the move towards the immobilisation of physical securities, which in

[26] Uncertificated Securities Regulations 1995, reg. 25.

English law means unregistered, or bearer, securities transferable by delivery of the instrument. An entire issue of securities can be immobilised at the time of issue, by deposit of a negotiable global note by the issuer; and holders of bearer securities may at any time immobilise them by delivering the relevant instruments to the depositary or custodian by way of transfer of ownership. The effect of immobilisation is, in the case of a new issue, that the investor's relationship is not with the issuer but with the depositary, and, in the case of deposit of securities already in issue, that the link between depositor and issuer is broken, the depositary becoming the holder. Where the global note is purely temporary, the investor acquires the right to have definitive bearer securities issued to him. Where the global note is permanent, the investor never, except in extreme circumstances, acquires the right to have definitive notes issued to him; his entitlement is recorded in an account with the depositary and takes the form of a right against the depositary to dividends, interest, redemption payments and the like, received by the depositary as note holder, so far as these receipts are attributable to the investor's beneficial interest in the note issue. The depositor of bearer securities transfers ownership of them and acquires a personal right, as the holder of a fungible securities account, to redelivery of securities of the same type and nominal value. Whether he also acquires a co-ownership interest in the pool of fungible securities held by the depositary depends on whether the latter is acting, in English law terms, as trustee or as banker, a crucial point which I shall develop. The account holder may himself hold his entitlement, wholly or in part, for the benefit of one or more clients. Their entitlements are in the nature of sub-interests; and just as the original investor has no relationship with the issuer, only with the depositary, so also the client of an investor holds this entitlement solely against the investor, not against the depositary or the issuer. These account interests, like any other intangible rights, may be transferred absolutely or given in security by means of book-entry in the accounts of the depositary or, in the case of sub-interests, of the party with whom the account is held.

Immobilisation has two great advantages. It avoids the risk, expense and inconvenience of moving large quantities of negotiable paper around the world; and in the case of immobilisation of a permanent global note it obviates the administration and cost involved in the issue of security-printed certificates. Immobilisation is an interesting example of the way in which the wheel so often turns full circle in the evolution of commercial practice. Having spent centuries reifying contract rights, and making them marketable, by embodying them in negotiable paper transferable by delivery, we are now moving away from transferable paper and back to contract rights. But a crucial question is whether the rights of the investor or depositor *are* purely contractual, in which case he carries the risk of insolvency of the depositary, or whether on the other hand he has a proportionate interest in the underlying securities held by the depositary, an interest that could be asserted against the depositary's general creditors.[27] It is clear that the depositor has no right to any specific securities. Whether he has an interest in the pool depends on the agreement between the parties and on the applicable law. Belgium and Luxembourg have both enacted legislation to ring-fence securities held by depositaries, so as to prevent them from being available to their general creditors. This is of particular importance in relation to the two international central securities depositaries, Euroclear and Cedel Bank. Luxembourg law is particularly interesting, for it provides a choice of method.[28] A depositor can be given a co-ownership interest from the beginning, or he can opt for an alternative procedure under which his rights against the depositary remain purely personal *until* the depositary's insolvency, in which event its holdings of deposited securities become ring-fenced and immune from the general body of creditors—a concept quite alien to English insolvency law but highly effective nevertheless, and possessing the advantage of allowing the depositary unrestricted dealing powers prior to bankruptcy. Outright transfers and pledges can be effected by book-entry in the records of the depositary. In the United States, Article 8 of the Uniform Commercial Code has been revised to provide a highly sophisticated treatment of rights derived from immobilised securities,

---

[27] This issue has attracted growing debate in England, as elsewhere, in recent years. See, for example, Kathleen Tyson-Quah, "Cross-Border Security Collateralisation Made Easy" (1996) J.I.F.B.L. 177; Roy Goode, "The Nature and Transfer of Rights in Dematerialised and Immobilised Securities", *ibid.*, at p. 167; and 'Cross-Border Securities Collateralisation: A Question of Jurisdiction", *ibid.*, at p. 410.

[28] See the comments of "PM" (Professor Paul Mousel) in (1996) J.I.F.B.L. 410 at p. 415.

and this has now been adopted in the majority of states in the Union, including the state of New York. Again, it is the account with the depositary that represents the source of the depositor's title, and if the depositor holds for clients of its own it is the entry in his books which is the source of their title.

In England there is as yet no legislation governing the point. The flexibility of our unwritten law enables co-ownership interests to be readily created by contract or by declaration of trust and allows derivative interests to be created by sub-trust. Does this mean that we can safely leave the legal treatment of rights relating to investment securities to be left to contract and rules of equity and trusts? I am in no doubt that this would be folly. It is indeed astonishing that we have managed so far without calamity. The acquisition of property rights is, it is true, sufficiently accommodated by the trust and the sub-trust, whilst the treatment of associated rights such as voting can usually be dealt with by contract or deed poll; but in other respects the common law either fails to provide clear answers or possesses priority rules which are ill-suited to this form of security. For example, primacy is given to a legal title acquired in good faith and without notice over a prior equitable title; but in the case of immobilised securities the account holder's interest takes the form of shared equitable ownership, so that legal title can never be acquired except by remobilising the security, and even this is rarely possible where what is deposited is a permanent global note. This is not without importance in that English law has no separate perfection requirement for a fixed charge on securities. They are not registrable under the Companies Act, and while we have regulations as to the transfer of title to dematerialised securities our statute law currently makes no provision for title through an account with a depositary of physical securities. Transfer into the name of the chargee would *de facto* give control to the chargee and notice to third parties, but if this is not done a subsequent chargee would appear bound by the prior charge, at any rate in the absence of some rule of estoppel.

Again, though English law recognises sub-mortgages and sub-pledges, the permissible terms of a sub-mortgage of an equitable co-interest in a pool of fungible securities have never been worked out. Is it sufficient if on the day the mortgagor seeks to redeem the mortgagee has the asset back in its hands, or is it necessary that the sub-mortgage shall by its terms be limited to the period of the head mortgage and that the amount secured shall not exceed that secured by the head mortgage? Further, it is necessary to deal with the position of sub-accounts and, for the efficient working of the system, to override the rule that a securities intermediary that honours a transfer instruction at a time when it has notice of a third party's rights incurs a liability to that party. Again, the Court of Appeal decision in *Macmillan*[29] that securities are deemed to be located in the country of issue and that transfers are governed by the law of that country is ill-suited to the transfer of interests in a fungible pool through the books of a depositary or securities intermediary. A better solution was that proferred by Millett J. at first instance,[30] namely the *lex loci actus*, which in most cases corresponds to the *lex situs* of the subject-matter of the transfer. For this purpose we have to identify the subject-matter of the dealing. Where it is the certificate itelf, the principle of transparency requires the application of the law of the place where the certificate is located at the time of transfer. But where (as will usually be the case where the certificate is immobilised in a depositary institution) the dealing is not in the certificate but in the rights derived from the account, it is the law of the location of that depositary or intermediary[31] that should govern. All this requires careful analysis and legislative treatment.

The fact that dealings in immobilised securities have distinctive features does not mean that we should jettison existing concepts, but they must be refashioned and qualified so as to produce workable solutions to typical problems. It has to be said that, compared with the enormous and effective efforts put into these problems by some of the best legal and business brains in America, resulting in a revised Article 8 of the Uniform Commercial Code, we in this country have barely begun to scratch the surface of the problems. What our law is having to accommodate is a marked shift from interests in *things* to interests in *bundles of rights*: a major challenge for the lawmakers of the 21st century.

---

[29] *Macmillan Inc. v. Bishopsgate Investment Trust plc* [1996] 1 W.L.R. 387.

[30] [1995] 1 W.L.R. 978.

[31] This could be the law of the place of incorporation (which, however, would not be appropriate for unincorporated bodies such as Cede & Co., the firm which holds securities on behalf of the Depositary Trust Corporation in New York) or, more satisfactorily, the place where the depositary or intermediary has its seat. A further alternative is the location of the record itself, but that is less suitable, for with modern technology it can be switched too readily to constitute a stable connecting factor.

IV ARE PROPERTY RIGHTS TOO EXPANSIVE?

I shall conclude by raising the question whether we have not carried the concept of proprietary rights too far. We have the principle of equity which converts uncompleted agreements for transfers into transfers, thus obliterating at a stroke the distinction between property and obligation in relation to an asset. We have global security and all-moneys retention of title clauses. We have express, implied, constructive and resulting trusts. There is even a call for the prepaying buyer to be given a constructive trust over the price paid to the seller pending delivery of the goods or services to which the payment relates.[32] If we go on like this all creditors will hold proprietary rights; and if everyone is thus secured the end result is exactly the same as if no one were secured.

It is now too late to roll back the map on most of these property principles, though I still entertain the hope that the courts will come round to the view that restitution should not be given for wrongs to the plaintiff (as opposed to improper removal or retention of his property) except on terms that adequately protect unsecured creditors. But it is necessary to balance proprietary rights against the legitimate concerns of ordinary trade suppliers; and what cannot be achieved by changing our principles of property law can in my view be attained through changes in insolvency law. In particular, we should resurrect the proposal made by the Cork Committee for the surrender by debenture-holders of 10 per cent in value of all assets subject to a floating charge so as to provide a fund available for unsecured creditors; and we should replace our preference rules, by which payments and transfers to a creditor can be set aside only if it is shown that the debtor company was influenced by a desire to improve the creditor's position, with new rules which apply an objective standard of unfair improvement, while on the other hand exempting payments and transfers made in good faith in the ordinary course of business.

---

[32] Indeed, in *Liggett v. Kensington* [1993] 1 N.Z.L.R. 257 the Court of Appeal of New Zealand held that the purchase price paid to acquire an interest in an undivided part of a bulk was impressed with a trust in favour of the buyer and, moreover, a trust subsisting from the outset. The decision was reversed by the Privy Council *sub. nom. Re Goldcorp Exchange Ltd* [1995] 1 A.C. 74, where the fallacy of the reasoning advanced by the court below was trenchantly exposed by Lord Mustill.

4. Commercial Law in an International Environment: Towards the Next Millennium

We have seen that the medieval law merchant, which was international in character, gradually became domesticated and displaced by national law, so that in the curriculum of the English law school the "law of international trade" refers not to the international law of trade but to the rules of English law governing cross-border trading transactions. This may have served us well enough when we had an Empire, when Britain ruled the waves and English commercial law and legislation were widely adopted throughout the common law world. But those halcyon days (viewed from the perspective of English law) are long since gone. The huge growth of international trade and the increasing interdependence of the major markets of the world have brought about a realisation of the importance of collaboration both in formal lawmaking and in the codification of trade usage. Within Europe the drive towards the integration of national laws is accelerating as the result of the creation of the European Single Market, and will be given further impetus by Directives associated with European Monetary Union.

The questions I wish to explore are the likely impact of these developments on the shape of English commercial law, the part that we can play, and already play, in influencing harmonising measures, and, finally, the adequacy of our commercial law, in substance and in form, to meet the challenges of the next millennium, or at any rate, of its beginning.

I THE INTERNATIONAL CONTEXT: PUBLIC LAW

Underlying the harmonising measures taken or in prospect in the public law field are three primary objectives. The first is the promotion of free and fair trade between nations, with the dismantling of national barriers to inter-state trade and the outlawing of laws and practices that distort markets. This is the province of international economic law, a huge area which deserves a lecture series to itself. I shall say no more about it tonight. The second is the financial stability of the markets and the avoidance of systemic risk, the risk that the failure of a major participant will have a domino effect, threatening the solvency of other players and ultimately of the market itself. The third, within the European Union, is promotion of the financial stability of Member States, and their closer political integration, through the introduction of European Monetary Union.

Protection of the markets

Governments have long been concerned to ensure the financial stability of their banks and other credit institutions. That this concern is well founded is adequately demonstrated by the collapse of a large number of secondary banks in the United States many years ago, of major failures in the Canadian banking system and, in our own country, the insolvency of BCCI and of Barings. Hence the adoption by the European Union of measures set out in the Basle Accord concerning credit institutions and, in particular, directives on capital adequacy, solvency ratios, own funds and the like. Meanwhile the European Central Bank and the national central banks are putting in place a European-wide system, known as TARGET, for real-time gross settlement of payment instructions. Under this system a bank proposing to send a payment instruction to another bank for the account of its customer will first send an online message to the Bank of England to make the necessary transfer from the sending bank's account to the receiving bank's account with the Bank of England. Only when this has been confirmed will the payment instruction be sent, by which time the receiving bank will know that it is already in funds to pay its customer. This avoids the daily exposure attendant on a netting system carried out at the end of the day, when a bank may be found to have incurred large liabilities that it is unable to meet. Real-time gross settlement will help to avoid a repetition of the débâcle caused by the collapse of the Herstatt Bank in 1974, which led to multiple lawsuits in a number of jurisdictions. The interdependence of world markets adds a new dimension to these concerns, for the IMF and central bankers now have to consider not only systemic risk within a particular national market but the domino effect of a collapse of one country's financial system on the stability of others, as so recently demonstrated by the financial crisis in the Far East.

But these and other measures, such as the attempt to introduce systems for delivery against payment in the securities markets, are addressed to what I would call factual risk. Of almost equal significance is legal risk; and in relation to operations conducted in a clearing system on an organised market, the most dominant legal risk is that arrangements for the netting out of obligations among participants will be struck down as contrary to insolvency law. That this was a real risk under English law was demonstrated by the majority decision of the House of Lords in *British Eagle*.[1] That case concerned a clearing house system set up by the International Air Transport Association by which sums due from member airlines to each other (*e.g.* for carrying each other's passengers) would be netted out each month, remittances being sent out by IATA to airlines that were net creditors and collected from airlines that were net creditors. British Eagle went into liquidation owing money to a number of airlines but with a claim against Air France which the liquidator sought to recover. Air France pleaded that the liquidator was bound by the rules of the clearing system and could only collect such sum, if any, as was due to it after the netting process had been completed. The liquidator argued that this contravened the principle of *pari passu* distribution on insolvency in that it removed from British Eagle's estate the sum due from Air France, which would otherwise have been available for all British Eagle's creditors, and gave a preference to airline creditors. This contention was upheld by a majority, while a strong minority insisted that the netting arrangements were commercially sensible and legitimate and that the liquidator could not take the benefit of the Air France contract without being subjected to the payment mechanism forming part of that contract.

There were other concerns, also about netting. For example, it was not clear that an entitlement to the future delivery of foreign currency could be set off against an accrued money obligation. This could be avoided by provisions allowing the

[1] *British Eagle International Airlines Ltd v. Compagnie Nationale Air France* [1975] 2 All E.R. 264.

delivery obligation to be closed out by a reverse transaction, thus converting it into a net money obligation, but only if this conversion took place before the advent of liquidation.

Such was the anxiety over the possible impact of these problems on clearing and settlement systems that in Part VII of the Companies Act 1989 provisions were introduced that, in effect, rendered all market contracts and all settlement or default rules of a recognised investment exchange or clearing house entirely immune from attack under insolvency law, and suspended rights of proof in the liquidation until completion of the netting process prescribed by such rules. At the time I felt that the Department of Trade and Industry had over-reacted to pressure from the City in giving unprecedented exemptions from insolvency law. But I was wrong. The disallowance of set-off under clearing house netting arrangements would cause such huge exposures as to place at risk the financial stability of the entire market. And if further evidence were needed, the E.U. Council is about to issue a directive to protect the efficacy of netting arrangements, and the finality of settlement, from attack under insolvency law. I mention this as a good illustration of the perception at international level of the need to sacrifice the interests of general creditors under insolvency law for the greater good of avoiding the unwinding of apparently settled transactions and the risk of systemic failure that could ensue.

Of course, regulators are concerned not only with the financial stability of markets but also with their integrity. Here somewhat different considerations arise. Every country is concerned to avoid adverse domino effects in an international market. What may be less clear to some countries is whether the same applies to safeguards for the integrity of the market. Is there a temptation for one country to set its regulatory framework at a relatively low level, with a view to securing a competitive advantage over markets in other countries? Or will a relatively high level of regulation have the same effect, by making investors feel more confident in the operations of the market? Should national regulators compete with each other, producing the prospect of regulatory arbitrage? Or should they collaborate so as to ensure that their policies converge?[2] It is to be hoped that the latter approach will prevail.

[2] See Edmund W. Kitch, "Competition Between Securities Markets: Good or Bad?" in *The Future for the Global Securities Market* (ed. Fidelis Oditah, 1996), Chap. 13.

European Monetary Union

On January 1, 1999 a new era dawns in Europe with the introduction of the euro as the legal currency of states participating in the European Monetary Union. In the ensuing three-year transitional period, notes and coins denominated in the old national currency will still be legal tender but only as euro units running in parallel with euros and cents. On and after January 1, 2002 all payment obligations will have to be expressed in euros, though old notes and coin remain legal tender for a further six months. The United Kingdom seems likely to join EMU early in the next century but in any event is strongly affected by it in that our banks will be processing payments and receipts in euros. Moreover, the Bank of England and the City law firms have been placing their huge expertise at the disposal of the European Commission and other bodies involved in monetary union with a view to ensuring that the issues of legal risk are properly addressed.

Supposing that we do join EMU, what are the legal implications? Of course, the introduction of a single currency is not purely, or even primarily, a legal issue. At the economic level it is designed to reduce inflation and transaction costs, eliminate currency risk within Europe, expedite funds transfers and, in consequence, enhance cross-border trade and increase the size of the single market. At the political level it represents a symbol of ever closer integration. Few things are perceived as more indicative of national sovereignty and identity than one's domestic currency, with its issue controlled by the national central bank. All this will change with EMU and the power over money supply will pass to the European Central Bank.

But there *are* legal implications, though these would seem to be relatively modest compared with the initial operational difficulties surrounding the introduction of EMU. The main concern has been to ensure the continuity of contracts expressed in ECUs or in a national currency.[3] A European Union Regulation provides for the automatic conversion of ECU obligations in legal instruments into euro obligations on a one-for-one basis[4] and of national currency obligations into euro obligations at a

---

[3] See Financial Law Panel, *Economic and Monetary Union: Continuity of Contracts in English Law*.

[4] Regulation 1103/97 (dated June 17, 1997), art. 2(1). The Regulation is made under Article 235 of the E.C. Treaty.

conversion rate to be fixed for each currency.[5] To ensure continuity of contracts the Regulation also provides that these conversions are not to have the effect of altering any terms of a legal instrument or of discharging or excusing performance, nor will they entitle a party unilaterally to alter or terminate such an instrument except so far as the parties have otherwise agreed.[6] In most cases this should work reasonably well so long as the relevant contract is governed by the law of an EMU state, though the basis of some contracts, such as European currency swaps, will disappear and will presumably cause such contracts to be converted into annuities. Potentially more troublesome is the case of a contract providing for payment in the national currency of an EMU state but governed by the law of a state outside the EMU. It seems likely that most states outside the EMU will apply the law of the EMU state as the *lex monetae*, the governing monetary law, to determine what now constitutes the euro equivalent of the designated national currency. It is a well-established principle of private international law that what constitutes a country's currency at the due time for payment is determined by that country's law, and in the case of an EMU country it will be the euro equivalent of the contractually designated currency on the basis of the official conversion rate. The traditional rule does not quite fit the ECU, which is not a currency at all, merely a unit of account, but can be applied to produce the same effect. Where the contract is governed by the law of a state outside the EMU the impact of this conversion on the parties' contractual obligations will be governed not by the euro directive but by the governing law. It is thought that in most cases the conversion itself will not have significant effects; what may be more of a problem is the disappearance of a national price reference, such as PIBOR, used in the contract.

So the legal problems arising from the replacement of national currencies by the euro are unlikely to be as significant as is commonly supposed. Nor are they novel. The same problem has arisen countless times in history when two or more independent states have come together to form a new state. In the words of Ecclesiastes, "there is no new thing under the sun".

---

[5] *ibid.*, art. 4. The conversion rates will be fixed by regulations made under Art. 1091(4) of the Treaty.
[6] *ibid.*, art. 3.

II THE INTERNATIONAL CONTEXT: PRIVATE LAW

The domestication of commercial law and the conflict of laws

One major effect of the nationalisation of the old law merchant was the development of private international law or, more accurately, the conflict of laws—rules of national law fashioned for disputes with an international element. These rules cover such matters as determination of the law governing the dispute, the courts that are to have jurisdiction, and the recognition and enforcement of foreign judgments. So if an English seller supplies goods to a French merchant to be shipped from Germany under a contract of sale made in Belgium, an English court will apply the conflict of laws rules of English law to determine, for example, whether the contract is governed by English, French, German or Belgian law. The matter is usually straightforward where the parties have chosen the law to govern their contractual relationship, for most countries are prepared to allow contracting parties a high degree of autonomy in choice of law. Things become more complex where the contract is silent on the applicable law. The courts then have to decide which is the most appropriate law to apply, and this is usually done by considering what law has the closest connection with the contract and its performance, and by the selection of a relevant connecting factor, such as the contractual place of the performance which is in issue or the place of business of the party whose performance is characteristic of the contract—in the case of a contract of sale, the seller's place of business.

The conflict of laws is now highly developed as a branch of jurisprudence but is increasingly seen as a necessary rather than an adequate mode of resolving disputes relating to cross-border transactions. There are many reasons for this. Since the conflict of laws is not international but forms part of each state's national law, its rules vary from state to state. This gives opportunities for a party to engage in forum shopping, for bringing his proceedings in the court of a country whose conflict of laws will lead to the application of the law of a state most favourable to the plaintiff's case. That particular problem can be surmounted by an international conflicts convention that harmonises the conflict of laws rules in a particular field, such as the Hague Rules on the Law applicable to the Sale of Goods. But other problems remain. In particular, the law will vary from one country to another, making it very difficult for the enterprise which is transacting business around the world to organise its affairs so that each country's laws will be complied with. There are wide differences in the philosophy governing commercial transactions. Common law countries on the whole adopt a *laissez-faire* approach, giving wide support to the principle of party autonomy. Some civil law jurisdictions, by contrast, are stricter and more paternalistic in character. They may have a leaning towards debtor protection over creditors' rights, and their laws may, for reasons of history or policy, be less receptive to the types of transaction for which banking and commerce perceive a need, such as non-possessory security or the acquisition of proprietary rights in future property. Finally, the application of conflict of laws rules leads to the application of a national law which is likely to have been fashioned primarily for domestic transactions.

The move towards harmonisation

For all these reasons, there has been an increasing movement away from the purely domestic law of international trade and towards what has become known as transnational commercial law, the corpus of law resulting from the harmonisation or convergence of national laws, whether by international convention, conscious or unconscious judicial parallelism, uniform rules for specified types of contract and, more recently, international restatements of principles of contract law such as those promulgated by Unidroit (the International Institute for the Unification of Private Law, the intergovernmental body set up in 1926 to work for the progressive harmonisation of private law) and the Commission on European Contract Law. But since it is not feasible to harmonise all commercial law, the conflict of laws will continue to play a significant role for the foreseeable future.

It is an interesting phenomenon that the impact of European Community law on the private rights of parties to commercial transactions, as opposed to transactions with consumers, has so far been almost negligible. If we leave on one side E.C. conventions of a general character, such as the Rome Convention on the law applicable to contractual obligations and the Brussels and related conventions on jurisdiction and the enforcement of judgments, it is hard to recall any measure of significance in the field of private commercial law other than the Directive on commercial agents,[7] which certainly introduced concepts novel to English law, such as the non-excludable right of a commercial agent to compensation or an indemnity on termination of his agency. So what we have is mainly a public law superstructure which, outside commercial agency, has not so far been under-pinned by any measures to harmonise, for example, the law of obligations or the law governing dealings in commercial assets.

In my view the European Union has been wise to exercise restraint in this regard, for there are other agencies whose remit is universal rather than regional and whose products are more focused on the private law of commercial transactions. I refer in particular to law-producing bodies such as Unidroit; UNCITRAL (the United Nations Commission on International Trade Law), established by the United Nations to advance and co-ordinate the harmonisation of international trade law; and the Hague Conference on Private International Law, the grand-father organisation that recently celebrated its centenary and produces conventions harmonising rules of the conflict of laws. Other international organisations serve specialist fields, such as shipping and aviation. Within the private sector the Inter-national Chamber of Commerce, the world representative of business, is far and away the most prominent and, not being a lawmaking body, makes its contribution in the form of uniform rules, customs and practices which are given effect by incor-poration into contracts.

Among the legal instruments that these bodies have pro-duced, pride of place must surely go to the United Nations Convention on Contracts for the International Sale of Goods. Concluded in Vienna in 1980, this convention, which possesses no fewer than 101 Articles, has now been ratified by 51 states and, in addition to its primary function of regulating the contractual rights and obligations of parties to international contracts of sale, has become the reference point for general provisions (for example, sphere of application and rules of interpretation) in smaller conventions in associated fields, such as the Unidroit conventions on international factoring and international financial leasing. Other significant existing or pro-spective legal instruments and model laws include the widely

---

[7] Directive 186/653 on the co-ordination of the laws of Member States relating to self-employed commercial agents (December 18, 1986).

adopted UNCITRAL Model Law on International Commercial Arbitration, its draft convention on the assignment of receivables and the Unidroit draft convention on international interests in mobile equipment. The latter is highly innovative and seeks to overcome the difficulty of perfecting security and related interests in equipment that is never stationary for very long in or over any jurisdiction, such as aircraft, space objects, oil rigs and railway rolling stock. This will be done by creating an entirely international interest which would be registered in an international register and would be given recognition and, within limits, priority and protection against the debtor's insolvency in all contracting states.

But international instruments such as conventions are not the only forms of transnational commercial law. The networking of contracts which incorporate uniform rules or uniform trade terms, such as those issued by the International Chamber of Commerce, produces effects which are at least as wide-ranging, if not more so. The ICC's Uniform Customs and Practice for Documentary Credits are used the world over, so that almost all international transactions in which payment is to be made under a documentary credit are likely to be subject to the same standard rules. Nor should the importance of local and international trade usage be overlooked. In some systems, including our own, trade usage is given effect as an implied term of the parties' contract. If they deal in a particular market they are presumed to contract with reference to the settled usages of the market. In other systems usages are considered to have independent normative force. I do not propose to engage in the debate on the existence of an autonomous international *lex mercatoria* save to say that I do not believe in it. I do, however, believe in the binding force of established usage as an implied term of contracts. Indeed, I will go further and say that, contrary to what one might suppose, trade usage is in practice a higher norm than an international private law convention, which typically is dispositive in character and yields to the contrary agreement of the parties, including terms implied from usage. This is expressly stated in, for example, the Vienna Sales Convention. The difficulty, of course, lies in identifying and proving the usage, particularly at international level. This is less easily done before courts than before arbitrators, who tend to adopt more relaxed standards of proof. A good example is furnished by *Libyan Arab Foreign Bank v. Bankers Trust*.[8] In that case:

> The plaintiffs held an account with the defendants in London denominated in U.S. dollars and had the right to call for transfer of further dollar funds on deposit with the defendants in New York. Relations between Libya and the United States became strained and the plaintiffs called on the defendants to transfer to London the whole balance available for transfer. The defendants delayed implementing this instruction and in the meantime an order was issued by President Reagan freezing all property and accounts held by the Libyan government and its agencies, including accounts held with overseas branches of American banks. Thereupon the plaintiffs made demand for payment of the sum held on deposit in Eurodollars in London and payment of the amount which should have been transferred from New York. The defendants said that they could not meet either demand. Transfer from the New York account would be unlawful under the Presidential Order. As to the London deposit it was, they said, established usage on the Eurodollar market that it was a non-cash market and that the transfer of funds denominated in dollars could be effected only through CHIPS, the New York clearing system. The plaintiffs for their part demanded the right to be paid in cash or by any method which did not involve activity in the United States.
>
> Staughton J. upheld the plaintiffs' claims and gave them judgment. The freeze order would not have affected the funds in New York if the defendants had honoured their instructions; and the plaintiffs were entitled to withdraw their London deposit in cash if they so chose. The usage contended for had been challenged by a banking expert and had not been established.

Now there was, it is true, a slight practical problem about withdrawal in cash in that the sum on deposit in London was $131 million dollars, and there were not enough dollar notes in London, or probably even in the whole of Europe, to cover that amount, so that it would be necessary to get the notes from a Federal Reserve Bank in the United States and send them by a fleet of aircraft to London! The defendants painted the pitiable spectacle of the time and expense it would take to count the notes when the highest denomination was U.S. $100. But the judge would have none of it. The plaintiffs were entitled to hard cash and to have it without payment of counting charges. In the

---

[8] [1989] Q.B. 728.

end the U.S. authorities approved payment of the judgment, thus avoiding the need for aircraft to be sent from the United States and for wheelbarrows stuffed with dollars to be pushed through the streets of London. I believe that on the evidence the judge was entirely right, though I suspect that an arbitral tribunal might have reached a different decision. Indeed, it is not always appreciated how much the dispute resolution method influences both the law that is applied and the overall substantive result.

Judicial parallelism is an increasing source of transnational commercial law and provides vivid examples of the way in which the approaches of courts of different countries to new ideas and new commercial instruments tend to converge in subordinating established doctrine to the needs of the market. Examples are not hard to find. In the mid-1970s our courts became aware that our doctrine of absolute state immunity, which prevented states from being sued even when they were acting in a commercial, rather than a sovereign, capacity, was out of line with the law of most other countries. In the characteristically graphic words of Lord Denning in *Trendtex*:

> "Seeing this great cloud of witnesses, I would ask: is there not here sufficient evidence to show that the rule of international law has changed? What more is needed? Are we to wait until every other country save England recognises the change? Ought we not to act now? Whenever a change is made, someone some time has to make the first move. One country alone may start the process. Others may follow. At first a trickle, then a stream, last a flood. England should not be left behind on the bank."[9]

This is a case of conscious borrowing of foreign law. An example of unconscious judicial parallelism is the recognition that abstract payment undertakings, such as letters of credit and demand guarantees are legally binding by virtue of their own issue. Courts throughout Europe have wrestled with the problem how to fit these undertakings, which are not supported by consideration or by *cause* in the normal sense, into orthodox contract doctrine. They have bent the rules to do it, recognising that this was essential to the efficacy of bank payment instruments in international transactions. Our courts would certainly

---

[9] *Trendtex Trading Corp. v. Central Bank of Nigeria* [1977] Q.B. 529.

do likewise, though curiously the question appears never to have arisen for direct decision. Again, we see replicated at the international level what is embedded in our own commercial law, namely the importance attached by the courts to upholding the reasonable practices of merchants.

Finally, I want to come back to the Unidroit *Principles of International Commercial Contracts* and its European counterpart, *Principles of European Contract Law*. These do not enjoy the force of law; they are in the nature of restatements of contract of the kind so successfully prepared by the American Law Institute in the United States. Their force is based on influence, not on power. Their impact has been quite remarkable.[10] The Unidroit *Principles*, which were first in the field after a long gestation period, have been the subject of countless articles and national and international conferences and seminars, and feature in courses and teaching materials of a great many law schools around the world. Many of their provisions have influenced revisions of the civil codes of a number of countries, including the Netherlands, Germany, the province of Quebec and, as regards its tentative draft contract code, New Zealand. The *Principles* have also been invoked in numerous actions and arbitral proceedings and even in judgments and awards as an international standard of contractual obligations. In this way they have become a kind of codified international *lex mercatoria* in the field of contract law. The *Principles of European Contract Law* have also been widely cited. What this heartening experience shows is that legal scholars have an important role to play in encouraging national courts to think internationally even when applying their own law to an international commercial dispute.

What emerges from all these developments is that with the enormous growth of cross-border trade it is no longer sufficient for a party to rely on his own national law, even where this is the law chosen to govern his contract, because no contract can lay down rules governing the priority of ownership and security interests as against third parties, still less can it secure the

---

[10] See M.J. Bonell, "The UNIDROIT Principles in Practice: The Experience of the First Two Years" [1997] 1 Uniform Law Rev. 34. Professor Bonell chaired the Unidroit Working Group which produced the Principles. They are extensively analysed in his commentary *An International Restatement of Contract Law* (2nd ed., 1997), which also reproduces the text in 10 languages.

efficacy of such interests on an insolvency in a foreign jurisdiction. It is therefore in the interest of bankers and of commerce and industry to join with governments in working towards the harmonisation of commercial law affecting the most important classes of transaction, such as international sales of goods, cross-border security, rules governing international payments, and the like.

English commercial law and the international scene

This brings to me the role of the United Kingdom in developing transnational commercial law. How influential is our own law? And how international is our outlook, how responsive are we to the calls for greater harmonisation of commercial law?

There seems little doubt that English commercial law is highly regarded by foreigners, who regularly select English law to govern their contracts and agree to submit their disputes to the English courts even where the transaction has no particular connection with this country. That is no doubt an acknowledgment of the pragmatism of English commercial law and its sensitivity to legitimate business needs and a tribute to the expertise of our judges and the efficiency of our systems for the resolution of commercial disputes. However, there are some serious problems. In the first place, our commercial law, consisting as it does of a number of archaic statutes bedded down on a mass of case law, does not lend itself to exportation, a matter to which I shall return. Foreign lawyers ask: where is your commercial code? Of still graver concern is our attitude towards the implementation of commercial law conventions. We make a considerable contribution to the preparation and content of conventions, but all too often, when the task is done, we walk away from the product, pleading a variety of excuses: the time is not ripe, there is insufficient support from industry and commerce, the legislative programme is too crowded. And it goes on being too crowded year after year, decade after decade. We seem unable to organise our affairs so as to reap the fruits of our own often arduous endeavours. So we steadily lose influence; our courts are largely deprived of the opportunity to contribute rulings on the interpretation of conventions, rulings which would be viewed with respect in other jurisdictions; and our traders, instead of being able to avail themselves of a neutral law hammered out among nations and available in English as an official text, find themselves subject to a foreign law which may be weighted heavily against them and may be expressed in a language they do not understand.

Nowhere is this chauvinistic approach better exemplified than in our attitude towards the Vienna Sales Convention. As stated earlier, this convention has now been ratified by no fewer than 51 states. With the exception of Japan they include most of the world's leading trading nations. But not the United Kingdom. After nearly two decades we have yet to ratify what has proved to be one of the world's most successful commercial law conventions, a convention to which distinguished United Kingdom lawyers made a major contribution. Why have we not joined? What is holding us back? It is hard to discern any rational policy objection to our ratification of the convention. The convention is permissive; almost all of it can be modified or excluded by the parties to suit their needs. So the convention does not impose on them anything they do not want. What the convention does is to provide parties neither of whom wishes to contract under the other's law with a set of neutral provisions which they can adapt as necessary. The convention also fulfils a second and important function, namely as a gap-filler to supply terms which the parties have not negotiated. Every day large numbers of contracts are being concluded informally, in a communication by telephone, fax or e-mail, where the bare essence of the transaction is agreed, leaving other terms to be settled later. This can cause problems if the supplementary terms are not in fact agreed. The convention will provide answers to most of these. It is not a comprehensive convention—it does not, for example, cover property rights—nor is it perfect, since it has to accommodate a wide range of different viewpoints. But it is for the most part a good deal better than our own Sale of Goods Act, to which I shall refer later; and it may serve the English party much better than a domestic foreign law to which that party might otherwise be subject. With 51 ratifications that do not include that of the United Kingdom, we are beginning to look faintly ridiculous. And why should we always be the ones to lag behind? Why cannot we give leadership and in so doing increase our influence on transnational commercial law?

I have referred to the lack of political time, to which one might add the lack of political will. But it would be unfair to lay all the blame at the door of government. What has become apparent over the years, and has been taken on board by the

harmonising agencies, is the necessity of involving both governments and interest groups in a harmonisation project from the
very beginning, so that they can have an opportunity to shape it
while it is still in its formative stage. It is also important to
promote wider discussion on draft texts as they emerge, so that
interested parties become conversant with the proposed convention and can offer their own contributions and expertise. And
here I should like to pay tribute to the sterling work of the
Business Law Unit of the Department of Trade and Industry.
The Unit has hosted several seminars on draft Unidroit and
UNCITRAL texts and has been very active in promoting a
greater awareness of these. I believe that the Unit will have an
increasingly important role to play in helping to lay the foundations for the United Kingdom's greater participation in these
international initiatives.

III   TOWARDS THE NEXT MILLENNIUM

What are the challenges for commercial law as we approach the
21st century? I have already referred to the importance of
harmonisation, whether in the form of hard law, such as an
international convention, or of contractually incorporated rules,
such as those issued by the ICC, or of so-called soft law, as
exemplified by the two international restatements of contract
previously mentioned. In this concluding part of the final
Hamlyn lecture I should like, first, to consider some of the legal
implications of new technology, secondly, to comment on the
changing approach to commercial dispute resolution, and,
thirdly, to offer some more general reflections on the present
shape of English commercial law.

Technological developments

In debates concerning the legal implications of an electronic
business environment there is an unfortunate tendency to over-
emphasise the technology and to assume that it automatically
changes everything so far as legal relationships are concerned.
This is a myth which I am anxious to dispel. Whether one is
dealing with electronic funds transfer, the dematerialisation or
immobilisation of securities or the use of electronic bills of
lading, it is necessary to ask why, if the message is broadly the
same, its legal significance should be affected by the medium

through which it is sent. My heart warmed to a member of the audience at an International Bar Association gathering in Vienna some years ago who asked what, conceptually, was the difference between a funds transfer effected as the result of communication across the ether and the delivery of a sack of notes or gold carried over the shoulder from one place to another. This is a very perceptive question and one that needs to be addressed. Of course, it can be said that there are legal instruments, such as a bill of exchange or a bill of lading, which depend for their legal efficacy on a writing and a signature. The shipping conventions, for example, all refer to a signed bill of lading. But what is really at stake is an authenticated message, and modern legal definitions of writing and signature allow for any medium of communication and any proper system of authentication so long as the message is capable of being reproduced in tangible form.[11] Moreover, even where it is necessary to interpret international conventions as requiring a physical, signed document,[12] in most cases the desired effects of those conventions can be achieved by a contractual incorporation of the convention rules, which will thus apply as terms of the contract.

What, then, is so special about the medium? Why should electronic transmissions necessitate different rules of law? These questions are worth asking because in many cases we find the same rules apply to electronic transactions as to written ones. For example, the basic concepts of payment and the revocability of a payment instruction remain unchanged, though some tweaking of the rules is needed and this is usually achieved by rules of the clearing house. But computer technology does have an impact on legal rules and legal risk. Copyright issues have to be considered. Rules must be devised to govern the payment

---

[11] See, for example, the 1988 Unidroit Convention on International Factoring, art. 1(4)(b) ("'notice in writing' includes, but is not limited to, telegrams, telex and any other telecommunication capable of being reproduced in tangible form"); and the 1996 UNCITRAL Model Law on Electronic Commerce, art. 6(1) ("Where the law requires information to be in writing, that requirement is met by a data message if the information contained therein is accessible so as to be usable for subsequent reference"). For a detailed study of the meanings and requirements of "writing" and "document" in English primary and subordinate legislation, see Chris Reed, *Digital Information Law* (1996), which examines the provisions in a wide variety of statutes and statutory instruments.

[12] A requirement which could be conveniently overcome by ratification of the 1996 UNCITRAL Model Law on Electronic Commerce. See n.11, above.

systems themselves, the rights and obligations of the parties and the allocation of risk where the system fails or is improperly accessed. The ease and speed with which large sums can be moved around the world in an electronic environment creates the potential for large-scale losses through fraud or system failure. There was a celebrated event many years ago in New York when a clearing bank appeared to become increasingly insolvent as the day drew to a close. It transpired that a computer, with the malignity of intent that characterised the last weeks of the master computer HAL in 2001, was debiting the bank with all its outflows but failing to credit it with its inflows. The problem was dealt with by deferring the daily settlement for a few hours, during which time the defect was rectified. But imagine the consequences if it had not been.

There are also public law implications of electronic trading, particularly in the field of regulation. Data protection has become an increasingly complex field; so also has the legal treatment of digital cash. Is a person who holds value in an electronic purse to be treated as a depositor for the purpose of the Banking Act because of his right to require the bank issuing the electronic value to redeem it? Probably not in most cases, but the issue continues to be debated. How is control to be exercised over regulated activities where these are conducted through the Internet? How are we to establish in which jurisdiction relevant acts have occurred? And what is the position if one of the ingredients of an offence is committed in this country and the other or others abroad? These are matters yet to be resolved; they add a new dimension to the task of the regulator.

The resolution of commercial disputes

So far tonight I have concentrated on substantive law. But as I have remarked earlier in this lecture series, the procedure for the resolution of commercial disputes is itself of vital importance. It is no use having legal rights if they cannot readily be enforced and if disputes cannot be fairly and expeditiously resolved. It is generally considered that our central courts—in particular the specialist Commercial Court and the more general courts of the Queen's Bench and Chancery Divisions—provide a good, often an excellent, service to commercial users. Even so, over time the delays and expense associated with litigation led to the growth of commercial arbitration. This was seen as fast, flexible, informal, private, relatively inexpensive and conducive to finality. This is still true of a considerable amount of arbitration, particularly in the commodities field. But it has to be said that much commercial arbitration has become almost indistinguishable from litigation. Arbitral proceedings, particularly with a three-person tribunal in an international arbitration, can be very protracted and a good deal more expensive than litigation. We do at least have the benefit of a modern Arbitration Act[13] ordered in a logical arrangement and expressed in plain English. The Act follows the spirit of the UNCITRAL Model Law more closely than had at one time been envisaged, though Scotland was still bolder in its adoption of the Model Law. Even so, there is much dissatisfaction with arbitration and a growing drift towards alternative dispute resolution methods, such as mediation and the mini-trial. In the early days of ADR experienced arbitrators were inclined to be dismissive, taking the rather lofty view that it would no doubt work well enough in family disputes but would be quite unsuited to disputes of a commercial character. That view is increasingly seen as misplaced and ADR is growing. It is a great deal quicker and cheaper. Of course, it may not be successful, but most hearings appear to end in agreement. Of equal importance is the fact that ADR is designed to be non-confrontational, to expose the real reason, rather than the ostensible reason, for the parties' disagreement and to offer the prospects of continuance of their relationship instead of the acceptance of its breakdown. Moreover, because ADR is not fettered by legal rights and remedies and can facilitate non-legal forms of relief, such as the offer of a substitute contract to the aggrieved party or the resuscitation of an agreement that has been legally ended. What the commercial community has not yet fully appreciated is the importance of laying down procedures in advance at the contract stage by which principals not previously involved in the handling of the dispute and with authority to negotiate are brought into discussions at an early stage with a view to avoiding a breakdown of the relationship rather than simply assuming the breakdown and alleviating its consequences. I have discussed this in more detail elsewhere.[14]

---

[13] Arbitration Act 1996.
[14] "Dispute Resolution in the 21st Century", the 1997 Alexander Lecture, delivered in the Old Hall, Lincoln's Inn on June 24, 1997 and reproduced in (1998) 64 *Arbitration* 9.

The present state of English commercial law

I have said that we need to become more outward-looking, more international in our approach to international conventions. But what of the internal state of English commercial law? How well placed are we to undertake the challenges of change as we enter the next millennium? Here I have to say that for many years now the judiciary seems to be have been more attuned than the legislature to the need to keep abreast of legal thought and dynamics in the international community. The courts have shown an ever-increasing readiness to look to patterns of judicial lawmaking in other legal systems for solutions to help resolve complex issues of legal policy. Law, like friendship, has to be constantly cultivated and regularly renewed. When I visit other common law countries, and in particular Canada and the United States, I am immensely impressed with their concern to keep their commercial law up to date and with the enormous energy and legal creativity which their academic and practising lawyers bring to bear to modernise and keep under regular review their laws governing commercial transactions. Pride of place must go to the American Uniform Commercial Code. Admittedly this is powerfully driven by the need for harmonisation among 50 jurisdictions, a motive power we lack; but it is clear that the Americans take the health of their law very seriously indeed. And when I return to England I feel, as always, uplifted by the remarkably high regard in which our judiciary is held but depressed by the state of our statute book and by our inertia and complacent belief in the innate superiority of English commercial law. I believe that at the legislative level we have shamefully neglected our commercial law for as long as I can remember.

To test this, let us take a look at our principal commercial statutes. The Sale of Goods Act 1979 largely re-enacts the Sale of Goods Act 1893, which was brilliantly drafted by Sir Mackenzie Chalmers but is now 104 years old. A charge over goods by a company is registrable under section 395 of the Companies Act 1985 where, had it been given by an individual, it would have been registrable as a bill of sale. To find this out it is necessary to resort to the Bills of Sale Acts 1878 and 1882, which are among the most exquisitely technical ever to have been enacted and can be fully interpreted only by reading literally hundreds of reported cases. Our legislation dealing with factors and mercantile agents is itself 108 years old. What of our negotiable instruments law? We do not have a negotiable instruments law. What we have is a statute passed in 1882, another of Chalmers' outstanding pieces of legislation, which, however, has hardly been touched since it was passed and does not cover any of the newer forms of instrument. So we have no statutory provisions to make clear what is assumed in the market place (I believe correctly) that such instruments as certificates of deposit, floating rate notes and bearer bonds are negotiable despite any uncertainty as to the amount to be paid and despite the fact that some of these kinds of instrument are expressed to be subject to the terms of trust deeds and the power of trustees.

How is it that we feel able to embark on the 21st century with commercial law statutes passed in the 19th? How can we seriously expect to confront the problems of modern commerce with legislation enacted in the era of the steam coach, which had to be preceded by a man with a red flag; when the aeroplane, television, the computer and spacecraft were all in the future? Our version of a well-known aphorism is: if it's broken, don't fix it! And as if this were not bad enough, there are whole areas of the law relating to commercial transactions on which we have virtually no legislation whatsoever: nothing on funds transfers or payment systems, nothing on indirect holdings of immobilised securities, nothing on warehouse receipts and no up-to-date and integrated treatment of documents of title generally. And we are the world's leading financial centre! As so often in so many areas, when Parliament is inert it is the courts that have to come to the rescue; and it is only because of the commercial awareness of our judges and the high standing they enjoy with foreigners that we are able to manage. Surely it is not too much to ask that commercial law statutes be reviewed at least once every 25 years; and when more than a century has elapsed without significant change, we can reasonably assume that it is time to replace the entire legislation and begin again.

> "Ah Love! Could thou and I with Fate conspire
> To grasp this sorry Scheme of Things entire,
> Would not we shatter it to bits—and then
> Re-mould it nearer to the Heart's Desire!"[15]

My strong preference is for a commercial code of the kind so successfully adopted throughout the United States. A

---

[15] *The Rubáiyát of Omar Khayyam* (trans. Edward Fitzgerald), 1st ed., stanza 73.

commercial code has many advantages.[16] It gathers together in one place the rules governing the major forms of commercial transaction and thereby makes the law accessible both to lawyers and to laymen. At present we have to resort to textbooks. Helpful those they may be, they are no substitute for a code, for within a given subject they analyse each principle and rule separately, so that these are diffused across the entire work and are not available to the reader in one place as with a code.

A commercial code is also an exportable product. Even if not taken over in its entirety, it can provide the inspiration for a modern commercial law elsewhere and particularly in developing countries and those that have moved or are moving to a market economy. A code integrates what are at present a disparate collection of statutes, unconnected to each other, replacing them with provisions which cover the field as a whole, in which each part is linked to the others and which are bedded down on a set of general provisions governing all transactions to which the code applies. The very process of preparing a commercial code helps to expose the inadequacies and inconsistencies of the present law and provides an opportunity for commerce, industry and finance to identify weaknesses and to suggest what is needed to overcome them. There are other benefits. Transactions could be conducted more efficiently, legal rules would be much more susceptible to developing business needs than they are now and much time currently spent in digging for particles of commercial law and then arduously assembling them into a coherent principle would be saved.

The preparation of a code would involve several years of effort and a not inconsiderable expense; but that is the price to be paid for a quality product and it is surely a price worth paying. We continue to suffer from false economies in the shape of quick fixes that come unstuck, of half-baked legislation in other areas which has to be corrected, of a philosophy which counts nothing as worth doing unless it can be done quickly and produce an immediate return. But if industry does not shirk at devoting huge sums of money and years of research to producing quality products, surely the lawmakers, for a fraction of the

---

[16] For a full development of this thesis, see Roy Goode, "The Codification of Commercial Law" (1986) 14 Monash Univ.L.Rev. 135. The Chairman of the Law Commission, Mrs Justice Arden, also stressed the advantages of codification in her 1997 COMBAR lecture, "Time for an English Commercial Code?".

cost, can do the same. But if such a project is to succeed it must engage the interest and the involvement not only of academic and practising lawyers but of businessmen in industry, commerce and finance. They must be willing to join the lawyers in such an enterprise, to put their shoulders behind the wheel and, having helped to produce the modern legislation we so desperately need, to urge on government the importance of enacting it.

My final plea is for a greater academic commitment to commercial law. We need more, many more, academic lawyers in the field than we currently possess. Particularly do we need young scholars of an inquiring turn of mind, interested in the workings of commercial practice as well as the development of theory, who can advance the boundaries of knowledge and take our students forward into the next age of commercial law. They will find a warm welcome not only from their colleagues but from practitioners, who are only too happy to share their expertise, and from the judges, who from the House of Lords downwards have, in recent years in particular, been generous in acknowledging the contribution of scholarly writings to their decisions. The academic community is in turn indebted to Bench and Bar for reasoned arguments and judgments which form the basis of much of our teaching and research and which often possess such a combination of creative thinking and intellectual rigour as to make some of us wonder if it is not the members of the practising profession who are often the true scholars!

We have come a long way from the ancient caravan trade and the medieval market, from the runner and the carrier pigeon to instantaneous global communication, from the longboat and the Phoenician round ship to the Japanese oil tanker, from dealings in physical assets to dealings in derivatives and other bundles of intangible rights. Yet the basis of our commerce remains as it was in early times: an organised, regulated market with an efficient clearing and settlement system, a procedure for the fair and expeditious resolution of disputes and a high degree of predictability of outcomes on issues of legal entitlement and obligation. It is a matter for some astonishment that although our legislation governing commercial transactions is archaic, foreigners continue to resort to English law and to English courts, while our own mercantile community remains able to structure agreements and relationships to produce almost any commercially desirable result, and to fashion new financial and commercial instruments, confident in the belief that these will be upheld and that the reasonable usages of merchants will be respected. But that is the genius of English commercial law.

*   *   *

At this point I would normally have sat down, as I have now concluded the 1997 Hamlyn Lectures. But through the indulgence of the Chairman of the Hamlyn Trustees I have been allowed to detain you for just a few more minutes. This is my last year at Oxford before I retire. Some years ago it came to my mind that I had not yet delivered my inaugural lecture, and I thought that to do this when I had already been here five years might seem a little quaint. And since no one I consulted could think of a term to describe a lecture halfway between an inaugural and a valedictory, I did not give one. So this last Hamlyn lecture is also, in a sense, a valedictory to Oxford.

Before coming here I spent 18 happy years at Queen Mary College, later Queen Mary and Westfield College, in the University of London. I owed my move from practice to the groves of academe to an American visiting professor at Queen Mary, who suggested I might be interested in a post that had suddenly become vacant there, and to Professor Roger Crane, who enjoys the unique distinction of having founded two law schools—Nottingham and Queen Mary. He was my mentor and to him I owe a debt of immense gratitude. I cannot think of anyone else who would have taken what I still regard as the hair-raising risk of putting forward for appointment to a chair at the University of London one who had not only never taught in his life but had never even been to university—a fact I have successfully concealed from generations of students over the past 26 years!

I came to Oxford with my wife in 1990 to a chair which ever since has been generously funded by the international law firm Norton Rose, to whom I should like to express my deep appreciation. My first thought was how different everything seemed. For one thing, I could not, and still cannot, fathom how the University is run or who runs it. I did discover that it is intensely democratic, and that this can be extraordinarily frustrating as a project on which one has set one's heart wends its leisurely way through one committee after another, not infrequently returning for revision and resubmission. But over the years I have come to love this place. I love it for its eccentricities, its intellectual vigour and the richness of its academic life; for its fierce independence, and its willingness to make huge sacrifices for adherence to principles it holds dear; and for the friendship and support it offers those who are interested in taking it. And in this I include the officers and other administrators of the University. Oxford is not driven by management. Its administration does not seek to impose its will on our scholars. Rather its sees its role as helping the members of the academic community and the faculties and departments to which they belong to achieve their scholarly aspirations. From my fellow academics in general, and my friends and colleagues in the Law Faculty in particular, I have received nothing but kindness and support; from them and from my students I have found myself greatly enriched, both intellectually and in friendships developed and mutual respect. I also owe a great debt to my college, St John's, and its President, Dr Hayes, for all the help and encouragement I have received over the years; and to my long-suffering secretary Judith Crowle, for her hard work and loyalty. So it is with a certain sadness, but also with a sense of fulfilment, that at the end of this year I shall hang up my hat—or, rather, my gown—though I shall continue to have some involvement in teaching and in the life of the faculty for as long as my colleagues are prepared to allow.

It remains only for me to express my thanks to the Trustees of the Hamlyn Trust once again for the privilege conferred on me in being invited to deliver the 1997 Hamlyn Lectures, and to all those who have come to listen to them.

INDEX

Index

Contract law—*cont.*
pacta sunt servanda, 31
party autonomy and, 32
performance,
assurance of future, 35–36
suspension of, 33–35
predictability and, 14–15, 32
strengths and weaknesses of, 32–38
suspension of performance, 33–35
trade usage as implied term, 90–91
Contractual lien, 10
Conventions,
implementation by U.K., 94–95
Court of Admiralty, *see also*
Admiralty law.
Commonwealth , under, 4–5
erorsion of jurisdiction, 4–5
Courts,
market and, 40, 42, 100
role of, 31
Criminal law,
proprietary rights in personal
property under, 59
Criminal sanctions, 52
Dematerialisation of securities, 7, 75,
78
Department of Trade and Industry,
Business Law Unit, 96
Derivatives, 7, 11
Disclosure,
moral duty as to, 13
rules, overkill, 50
Discretions,
rules and, 49–52
Dishonest behaviour,
equitable rules, 21
Disintermediation, 39
Dispositive law,
pre-eminence of, 10–11
Dispute resolution,
alternative dispute resolution, 10,
99
arbitration, 98–99
choice of English law for, 11
English courts, in, 98–99
importance of procedures, 98
Doctors' Commons, 4
Economic activity,
commercial law, relationship
with, 4

Economic efficiency,
concept of, 28, 29
Economic loss, liability for,
concurrence of liability in contract
and tort, 22
generally, 9
professionals and third parties
and, 22–23
rules versus standards and, 22–24
Economic theory
role in shaping commercial law,
28–29
Electronic business environment,
legal implications of, 96–98
Electronic funds transfers, 7
Electronic purse, 7
English commercial law,
academic commitment, need for,
103
commercial code, need for, 101–103
development of, 4 *et seq.*
eminence of, 5–7, 94
exportation of, 94, 102
law reform, 28, 37–38
present state of, 100–104
transnational commercial law, role
in developing, 94–96
Entrepreneurial activity,
eminence of English commercial
law and, 5–6
flexibility/responsiveness of legal
system and, 6, 10
Equity,
boundaries of, 18–21
commercial law, relationship with,
9, 11, 13, 17–24
contract, relationship with, 9–10
dishonest behaviour rules, 21
fiduciaries and, 18–21, 42
predictability and, 17, 21–22
proprietary rights, 21
remedies, 42
role of, 18
rules versus standards and, 17–22
Ethics, *see also* Morality.
banking, 48–49
influence on law, 12
law influencing, 12
self-regulated markets and, 48–49
European Monetary Union, 85–86

109

Index